Israel: AN ECHO OF ETERNITY

Abraham Joshua Heschel is the author of

A PASSION FOR TRUTH

ISRAEL: AN ECHO OF ETERNITY

THE INSECURITY OF FREEDOM

WHO IS MAN?

THEOLOGY OF ANCIENT JUDAISM
    (*two volumes*)

THE SABBATH

THE EARTH IS THE LORD'S

MAN'S QUEST FOR GOD

GOD IN SEARCH OF MAN

MAN IS NOT ALONE

MAIMONIDES

ABRAVANEL

THE QUEST FOR CERTAINTY IN
    SAADIA'S PHILOSOPHY

THE PROPHETS

THE WISDOM OF HESCHEL

Israel:

AN ECHO OF ETERNITY

Abraham Joshua Heschel

Drawings by ABRAHAM RATTNER

Farrar, Straus and Giroux

New York

First edition, 1969
Eighth printing, 1987

My appreciation is due to the Anti-Defamation League of B'nai B'rith
and particularly to Miss Judith Herschlag for their assistance in making
this publication possible.

DESIGNED BY MARSHALL LEE

For Zion's sake I will not keep silent,
  and for Jerusalem's sake I will not rest,
until her vindication goes forth as brightness,
  and her salvation as a burning torch.
The nations shall see your vindication,
  and all the kings your glory;
and you shall be called by a new name
  which the mouth of the Lord will give.
You shall be a crown of beauty in the hand of the Lord,
  and a royal diadem in the hand of your God.
You shall no more be termed Forsaken,
  and your land shall no more be termed Desolate;
but you shall be called My delight is in her,
  and your land Married;
for the Lord delights in you,
  and your land shall be married.
For as a young man marries a virgin,
  so shall your sons marry you,
and as the bridegroom rejoices over the bride,
  so shall your God rejoice over you.
Upon your walls, O Jerusalem,
  I have set watchmen;
all the day and all the night
  they shall never be silent.

You who put the Lord in remembrance,
  take no rest, and give him no rest
  until he establishes Jerusalem
  and makes it a praise in the earth.
The Lord has sworn by his right hand
  and by his mighty arm: "I will not again give your
      grain
  to be food for your enemies,
and foreigners shall not drink your wine
  for which you have labored;
but those who garner it shall eat it
  and praise the Lord,
and those who gather it shall drink it
  in the courts of my sanctuary."

Isaiah 62:1–9

Contents

1. *Jerusalem—a charismatic city*

YOU ONLY SEE WHEN YOU HEAR   5

THE INTIMATION OF AN ANSWER   9

THE WIDOW IS A BRIDE AGAIN   14

THE WALL   19

CITY IN TRANCE   28

THE CHALLENGE   33

2. *Engagement to the land*

TO REPUDIATE THE BIBLE?   43

THE BIBLE IS OUR DESTINY   45

THE ECLIPSE OF THE BIBLE   47

SINGULARITY   49

THE DRAMA   52

CONTINUOUSLY ASSERTING OUR RIGHT   54

IN DIALOGUE WITH THE LAND   58

MEMORY   60

DWELLING IN THE LAND   67

EMISSARIES   85

3.   *Between hope and distress*

HOPE   93

WAITING   96

PROMISE   99

DISTRESS   104

THE MIRACLE OF THE RESURRECTION   109

DISASTER   111

PIONEERS   115

THE LAND   119

4.   *Israel and meaning in history*

MEMORY OF HISTORY   127

HISTORY IS NOT CONSUMED   131

LIVING TOWARD REDEMPTION   134

MOUNT SINAI AND MOUNT MORIAH   136

THE ALLEGORIZATION OF THE BIBLE   139

BODY AND SPIRIT   145

IMMEDIACY OF MEANING   148

5.   *Jews, Christians, Arabs*

TWO LEVELS OF REDEMPTION   155

THE CHRISTIAN APPROACH   161

ISLAM AND THE LAND OF ISRAEL   168

ARABS AND ISRAEL   173

6. *A rendezvous with history*

A RENDEZVOUS WITH HISTORY   195

REMEMBER   200

A RE-EXAMINATION   202

A SPIRITUAL UNDERGROUND   205

GRATITUDE   208

A COMMUNITY OF CONCERN   211

PEACE   213

MEANING   219

INDEX   227

1
Jerusalem—
a charismatic
city

Streams of endless craving, clinging, dreaming, flowing day and night, midnights, years, decades, centuries, millennia streams of tears, pledging, waiting from all over the world, from all corners of the earth carried us of this generation to the Wall.

ABRAHAM JOSHUA HESCHEL

YOU ONLY SEE WHEN YOU HEAR

July, 1967 . . . I have discovered a new land. Israel is not the same as before. There is great astonishment in the souls. It is as if the prophets had risen from their graves. Their words ring in a new way. Jerusalem is everywhere, she hovers over the whole country. There is a new radiance, a new awe.

The great quality of a miracle is not in its being an unexpected, unbelievable event in which the presence of the holy bursts forth, but in its happening to human beings who are profoundly astonished at such an outburst.

My astonishment is mixed with anxiety. Am I worthy? Am I able to appreciate the marvel?

I did not enter on my own the city of Jerusalem. Streams

of endless craving, clinging, dreaming, flowing day and night, midnights, years, decades, centuries, millennia, streams of tears, pledging, waiting—from all over the world, from all corners of the earth—carried us of this generation to the Wall. My ancestors could only dream of you—to my people in Auschwitz you were more remote than the moon, and I can touch your stones! Am I worthy? How shall I ever repay for these moments?

The martyrs of all ages are sitting at the gates of heaven, having refused to enter the world to come lest they forget Israel's pledge given in and for this world:

> *If I forget you, O Jerusalem*
> *let my right hand wither.*
> *Let my tongue cleave to the roof of my mouth*
> *if I do not remember you*
> *if I do not set Jerusalem*
> *above my highest joys.*

Psalm 137:5–6

They would rather be without heaven than forget the glory of Jerusalem. From time to time their souls would leave the gates of heaven to go on a pilgrimage to the souls of the Jewish people, reminding them that God himself is in exile, that He will not enter heavenly Jerusalem until His people Israel will enter Jerusalem here.[1]

---

[1] Zohar, I, 1b.

Jerusalem! I always try to see the inner force that emanates from you, enveloping and transcending all weariness and travail. I try to use my eyes, and there is a cloud. Is Jerusalem higher than the road I walk on? Does she hover in the air above me? No, in Jerusalem past is present, and heaven is almost here. For an instant I am near to Hillel, who is close by. All of our history is within reach.

Jerusalem, you only see her when you hear. She has been an ear when no one else heard, an ear open to prophets' denunciations, to prophets' consolations, to the lamentations of ages, to the hopes of countless sages and saints; an ear to prayers flowing from distant places. And she is more than an ear. Jerusalem is a *witness*, an echo of eternity. Stand still and listen. We know Isaiah's voice from hearsay, yet these stones heard him when he said concerning Judah and Jerusalem (2:2–4):

> *It shall come to pass in the latter days . . . .*
> *For out of Zion shall go forth Torah,*
>   *and the word of the Lord from Jerusalem. . . .*
> *He shall judge between the nations,*
>   *and shall decide for many peoples; . . .*
> *nation shall not lift up sword against nation,*
>   *neither shall they learn war any more.*

Jerusalem was stopped in the middle of her speech. She is a voice interrupted. Let Jerusalem speak again to our people, to all people.

7

The words have gone out of here and have entered the pages of holy books. And yet Jerusalem has not given herself away. There is so much more in store. Jerusalem is never at the end of the road. She is the city where waiting for God was born, where the anticipation of everlasting peace came into being. Jerusalem is waiting for the prologue of redemption, for new beginning.

What is the secret of Jerusalem? Her past is a prelude. Her power is in reviving. Here silence is prediction, the walls are in suspense. It may happen any moment: a shoot may come forth out of the stock of Jesse, a twig may grow forth out of his roots . . . .

This is a city never indifferent to the sky. The evenings often feel like Kol Nidre nights. Unheard music, transfiguring thoughts. Prayers are vibrant. The Sabbath finds it hard to go away.

Here Isaiah (6:3) heard:

Holy, holy, holy is the Lord of hosts:
the whole earth is full of His glory.

No words more magnificent have ever been uttered. Here was the Holy of Holies.

Jerusalem has the look of a place that is looked at . . . "the eyes of the Lord your God are always upon it, from the beginning of the year to the end of the year" (Deuteronomy 11:12). Psalms inhabit the hills, the air is hallelujah. Hidden harps. Dormant songs.

THE INTIMATION OF AN ANSWER

A necessary condition affecting human beliefs in philosophy and religion is the paradox. The source of their paradoxical character has its origin in the essential polarity of human being, e.g., in the opposition between unconditional truth and man's necessarily conditional perception of truth, in the opposition of unity and multiplicity, of the general and the particular, of the universal and the individual.

All men are created equal, yet no two faces are alike. All days can be defined in the same way—the period of the earth's revolution around its axis—yet the Sabbath is conceived in a special way. We are called upon to respect all human beings, yet are also called upon to revere our parents in a special way.

The chief difference between common sense and philosophical doctrine may be said to be "that the philosopher by his finer analysis, reveals the paradoxes which our everyday consciousness veils by means of a more or less thoughtless traditional phraseology. The philosopher is more frank with his antithesis. He does not invent the paradoxes; he confesses them."[2] To ignore the paradox is to miss the truth.

King Solomon in his speech inaugurating the Temple said: "The Lord dwells in thick darkness."[3] Will he dwell in a Temple? Will God indeed dwell on the earth? Behold heaven and the highest heaven cannot contain Thee, how much less the house which I have built?"[4]

"Do I not fill heaven and earth? says the Lord" (Jeremiah 23:24). "The whole earth is full of His glory" (Isaiah 6:3). Yet, although the Shekinah, the Presence, is everywhere, the experience of the Shekinah is always somewhere, because man always lives at a particular place in space.

Living truth is the blending of the universal and the individual, of idea and understanding, of distance and intimacy, the ineffable and the expressible, the timeless and the temporal, body and soul, time and space.

[2] Josiah Royce, *Lectures on Modern Idealism* (New Haven: Yale University Press, 1919), p. 93.
[3] I Kings 8:12: "Then Solomon said, 'The Lord has set the sun in the heavens,/but has said that he would dwell in thick darkness.'"
[4] Cf. I Kings 8:27.

10

Even those who believe that God is everywhere set aside a place for a sanctuary. For the sacred to be sensed at all moments everywhere, it must also at this moment be somewhere.

At the beginning is the moment, time, God's presence, holiness in time, the Seventh Day.

When history began, there was only one holiness in the world, holiness in time. When at Sinai the word of God was about to be heard, a call for holiness in *man* was proclaimed: "Thou shalt be unto me a holy people." It was only after the people had succumbed to the temptation of worshipping a thing, a golden calf, that the erection of a Tabernacle, of holiness in *space*, was commanded. The sanctity of time came first, the sanctity of man came second, and the sanctity of space last. Time was hallowed by God; space, the Tabernacle, was consecrated by Moses . . . .

The ancient rabbis discern three aspects of holiness: the holiness of the Name of God, the holiness of the Sabbath, and the holiness of Israel. The holiness of the Sabbath preceded the holiness of Israel. The holiness of the land of Israel is derived from the holiness of the people of Israel. The land was not holy at the time of Terah or even at the time of the Patriarchs. It was sanctified by the people when they entered the land under the leadership of Joshua. The land was sanctified by the people, and the Sabbath was sanctified by God.[5]

[5] Abraham J. Heschel, *The Sabbath* (New York: Farrar, Straus & Company, 1951), pp. 9 f., 81 f.

11

Jerusalem is "the city where I have chosen to put my name";[6] "the city of our God which God establishes for ever";[7] the city of prophecy.[8]

On the holy mount stands the city he founded;
  the Lord loves the gates of Zion
  more than all the dwelling places of Jacob.
Glorious things are spoken of you,
  O city of God. . . .
And of Zion it shall be said,
  "This one and that one were born in her";
  for the Most High himself will establish her. . . .
Singers and dancers alike say,
  "All my springs are in you."

                                        Psalm 87:1–7

God has chosen Jerusalem and endowed her with the mystery of His presence; prophets, kings, sages, priests made her a place where God's calling was heard and accepted. Here lived the people who listened and preserved events in words—the scribes, the copyists.

There are moments in history which are unique, mo-

---

[6] "Yet to his son I will give one tribe, that David my servant may always have a lamp before me in Jerusalem, the city where I have chosen to put my name" (I Kings 11:36).
[7] "As we have heard, so have we seen in the city of the Lord of hosts, in the city of our God, which God establishes for ever" (Psalm 48:8).
[8] Midrash on Lamentations, Proems, 22.

12

ments which have tied the heart of our people to Jerusalem forever.

These moments and the city of Jerusalem were destined to radiate the light of the spirit throughout the world. For the light of the spirit is not a thing of space, imprisoned in a particular place. Yet for the spirit of Jerusalem to be everywhere, Jerusalem must first be somewhere.

It was almost cruel. No image, no likeness, no icon of God! No man can see God and live. God, why not be considerate and show us Thy face? Thy justice is hidden, why should not Thy face be revealed?

Jerusalem is comfort, intimation of an answer.

History is not blind. The world is an eye, and Jerusalem corresponds to the pupil of the eye,[9] of an asking, discerning eye.

It was in Jerusalem where the prophet proclaimed: "And he will destroy on this mountain the covering that is cast over all peoples, the veil that is spread over all nations. He will swallow up death for ever, and the Lord God will wipe away tears from all faces, and the reproach of his people he will take away from all the earth; for the Lord has spoken" (Isaiah 25:7–8).

[9] *Derekh Erets Zutta*, ch. 9.

13

THE WIDOW IS A BRIDE AGAIN

Jerusalem is not divine, her life depends on our presence. Alone she is desolate and silent, with Israel she is a witness, a proclamation. Alone she is a widow, with Israel she is a bride.

Where is God to be found?

God is no less here than there. It is the sacred moment in which His presence is disclosed. We meet God in time rather than in space, in moments of faith rather than in a piece of space. The history of Jerusalem is endowed with the power to inspire such moments, to invoke in us the ability to be present to His presence.

I did not enter the city of David to visit graves or to gaze at shrines. I entered in order to share cravings welled up here, to commune with those who proclaimed and with those who preserved the words we now read in the Book of Books; with those who declared as well as with those who persevered in teaching us trust.

Here was no waste of history. Here you discover the

14

immortality of words, the eternity of moments. Wherever I walk in Jerusalem I am near a world in a state of trance, near a stillness that shelters eternity.

Throughout the ages the world considered us odd for taking the Hebrew Bible seriously, for trusting the prophets' words. God's promise to Abraham, Isaac, Jacob; to Amos, Hosea, Isaiah, Micah, Jeremiah, Ezekiel, remains strong and alive in our souls.

Zion is not a symbol, but a home, and the land is not an allegory but a possession, a commitment of destiny. How can anyone expect us to betray our pledge: "If I forget you, O Jerusalem, let my right hand wither" (Psalm 137:5)?

Jerusalem to the prophet is the quintessence of the land, corresponding to the people. "Comfort, comfort my people, says your God. Speak tenderly to Jerusalem . . ." (Isaiah 40:1–2). . . . "For the Lord has comforted His people, He has redeemed Jerusalem" (Isaiah 52:9). . . . "I will rejoice in Jerusalem and be glad in my people" (Isaiah 65:19).

Jerusalem is called the mother of Israel,[10] and she is also used as a synonym for Israel.

"We have never left Jerusalem, we have never abandoned the city of David. For thy servants hold her stones dear and have pity on her dust" (Psalm 102:15).

---

[10] Baruch 4:9; The Apocalypse of Baruch (II Baruch) 3:1; Yalkut Hamakizi, Psalm 147:4.

15

Jerusalem, the mother of Israel, we enter your walls as children who have always honored you, who have never been estranged from you. Your weight has been weighed in tears shed by our people for nearly two thousand years. Laughter was suppressed when we thought of your being in ruins. You are not a shrine, a place of pilgrimage to which to come, and then depart. "Wherever I go, I go to Jerusalem," said Rabbi Nahman.

Jerusalem, all our hearts are like harps, responsive when your name is mentioned.

Jerusalem, our hearts went out to you whenever we prayed, whenever we pondered the destiny of the world. For so many ages we have been love-sick. "My beloved is mine, and I am his," Jerusalem whispered. We waited through unbearably long frustration and derision.

In our own days the miracle has occurred. Jerusalem has proclaimed loudly: "My beloved is mine, and I am his!"

What happened on June 7, 1967? God's compassion has prevailed. So many devastations. Thousands of communities wiped out. Synagogues burned, people asphyxiated. No tombstones, no graves, all monuments meaningless.

In its solitude the Wall was forced into the role of an unreachable tombstone for the nameless dead. Suddenly the Wall, tired of tears and lamentations, became homesick for song. "O Come, let us sing to the Lord, let us chant in joy to the rock of our salvation!" (Psalm 95:1). It will be called the Rejoicing Wall.

16

> *Break forth together into singing,*
>   *you waste places of Jerusalem;*
> *for the Lord has comforted his people,*
>   *He has redeemed Jerusalem.*
> *The Lord has bared his holy arm*
>   *before the eyes of all nations;*
> *and all the ends of the earth shall see*
>   *the salvation of our God.*

Isaiah 52:9–10

We have arrived at a beginning; the night often looked interminable. Amalek was Führer, and Haman prevailed.

For centuries we would tear our garments whenever we came into sight of your ruins. In 1945 our souls were ruins, and our garments were tatters. There was nothing to tear. In Auschwitz and Dachau, in Bergen-Belsen and Treblinka, they prayed at the end of Atonement Day, "Next year in Jerusalem." The next day they were asphyxiated in gas chambers. Those of us who were not asphyxiated continued to cling to Thee. "Though he slay me, yet I will trust in him" (Job 13:15). We come to you, Jerusalem, to build your ruins, to mend our souls and to seek comfort for God and men.

We, a people of orphans, have entered the walls to greet the widow, Jerusalem, and the widow is a bride again. She has taken hold of us, and we find ourselves again at the feet of the prophets. We are the harp, and David is playing.

Spiritually I am a native of Jerusalem. I have prayed here all my life. My hopes have their home in these hills.

You will not understand what Jerusalem means in terms of generalizations or comparative history.

Jerusalem, we were forced to leave when driven out by conquerors, but we never abandoned, never relinquished you. Our parting was a pain to which we would never reconcile ourselves.

"The site has been captured, occupied, and recaptured by various people since the Old Stone Age and the Pleistocene period. During the past 3,500 years it has been held by Egyptians, Jebusites, Jews, Babylonians, Romans, Arabs, Turks, Britons, and now Jews again," writes the *Christian Century* without realizing that if Jerusalem had been only the city of Jebusites, Turks, and Arabs, there would have been no Christian century.

THE WALL

The Wall . . . At first I am stunned. Then I see: a Wall of frozen tears, a cloud of sighs.

Palimpsests, hiding books, secret names. The stones are seals.

The Wall . . . The old mother crying for all of us. Stubborn, loving, waiting for redemption. The ground on which I stand is Amen. My words become echoes. All of our history is waiting here.

No comeliness to be acclaimed, no beauty to be relished. But a heart and an ear. Its very being is compassion. You stand still and hear: stones of sorrow, acquaintance with grief. We all hide our faces from agony, shun the afflicted. The Wall is compassion, its face is open only to those smitten with grief.

So tough, so strong, so tenacious. How she survived the contempt of ages! For centuries while garbage was heaped in her front to cover her face, she remained impervious to

19

desecration, mighty, of mysterious majesty in the midst of scorn.

So many different rulers held sway over the city, so many cataclysmic changes, so many upheavals, so many eruptions of passion came to pass—the Wall kept a silent watch. ". . . a thousand years in thy sight are but as yesterday when it is past, or as a watch in the night" (Psalm 90:4).

"Behold, I made him a witness to the peoples" (Isaiah 55:4). These stones have a heart, a heart for all men. The Wall has a soul that radiates a presence.

When Jerusalem was destroyed, we were driven out and like sheep have gone astray; we have turned every one to his own way. The Wall alone stayed on.

What is the Wall? The unceasing marvel. Expectation. The Wall will not perish. The redeemer will come.

Silence. I hug the stones; I pray. O, Rock of Israel, make our faith strong and Your words luminous in our hearts and minds. No image. Pour holiness into our moments.

The Wall is silent? For an instant I am her tongue. Then I hear: I am a man of unclean lips. . . . O God, cleanse my lips, make me worthy to be her tongue. Forgive me for having tried to be her tongue for one instant. Forgive my ecstasy.

I am afraid of detachments, of indifference, of disjunctions. Since Auschwitz my joys grieve, pleasures are mixed with vexations.

20

No security anywhere, any time. The sun can be a nightmare, humanity infinitely worse than a beast. How to be in accord with Isaiah? I ask in my prayers.

Suddenly ancient anticipations are resurrected in me. Centuries went and came. Then a moment arrived and stood still, facing me.

Once you have lived a moment at the Wall, you never go away.

How can I depart from you? You have become a part of me. My bones will forever be filled with your secret.

I walk in the streets of Jerusalem recalling sorrow, nights of agony, nights of grief, nights of the ninth of Av. The reading of the Lamentations. The house of prayer is a house of weeping. It is the night on which God himself set fire to the first Temple and then to the second Temple.

> *He is to me like a bear lying in wait,*
> *   like a lion in hiding;*
> *he led me off my way and tore me to pieces;*
> *   he has made me desolate;*
> *he bent his bow and set me*
> *   as a mark for his arrow.*
> *He drove into my heart*
> *   the arrows of his quiver;*
> *I have become the laughingstock of all peoples,*
> *   the burden of their songs all day long.*

21

He has filled me with bitterness,
  he has sated me with wormwood.
He has made my teeth grind on gravel,
  and made me cower in ashes;
my soul is bereft of peace,
  I have forgotten what happiness is; . . .

Lamentations 3:10–17

All the glory is gone: the Temple, the Ark, Menorah, the Tablets. The people in captivity, Jerusalem in ruins. Only dust and stones remain. And we cherish the stones.

"How much longer shall there be weeping in Zion and mourning in Jerusalem?" asked Rabbi Abraham Ibn Ezra.

This is the city of David, of the prophets of Israel—not of Titus, the Roman Emperor; or of Godfrey of Bouillon, the Crusader; or of Saladin. The descendants of Titus, of Godfrey, of Saladin never fasted, never mourned for her. Jerusalem was not a part of their soul, of the grief, not an answer to their suffering.

The ninth of Av . . . We are a people in mourning, painfully puzzled, exceedingly forthright, but neither blasphemous nor bitter. What audacity in a soul that can ardently adore God and also say of Him: He was "like a bear lying in wait, like a lion in hiding. . . . The Lord has become like an enemy" (Lamentations 2:10,5).

22

We are a people in mourning but not in despair; overcome with grief but devoid of self-pity; lamenting disaster,
recollecting sins, self-impeaching. Mourning is repentance.
We are a people in a mourning that calls for mending.

Such deep sorrow is cleansing. It is a nondeliberate way
of expanding compassion, of understanding the nonfinality
of current history. Lamentation leaves behind an echo in
all our laughing. Yet that deep sorrow is also experienced
as a prelude to redemption.

We are a people in mourning, and so Erets Israel (land
of Israel) is a land in mourning. Our scars are her ruin.
Our affliction is her desolation. The soil does not respond.
The land is wrecked. We have misery in common.

During our annual penitential season we read a Selicha
—a penitential prayer written by Rabbi Gershom, Light of
the Exile (d. 1028):

> *The People: Captivity after captivity,*
> *All Judah is in captivity,*
> *Ever woebegone and pining away,*
> *No one cares or inquires after her.*

> *The Land: The Holy City and its countries*
> *Are for mockery and plunder,*
> *All her treasures are spoiled and*
> *vanished,*
> *Nothing remains save the Torah alone.*

My acquaintances mock me;
What hope gives you strength, you contemptible
    beggars?
If once you were children, beloved and cherished,
Now you are cast off like a potsherd, like homeless
    dogs!
How long will you foolishly wait for the end of
    Galut?
Are you not yet convinced that your hope is a mad
    vanity?

We, a people in mourning, are not alone in our grief. With us Zion and Jerusalem are in mourning. These are the words we pray on the ninth day of the month of Av.

O Lord, our God, comfort the mourners of Zion and mourners of Jerusalem, the city that is in mourning, laid waste, despised and desolate.

She is in mourning because she is without her children; she is laid waste, in her dwellings; despised, because of the downfall of her glory; desolate, because of the loss of her inhabitants.

She sits with her head covered like a barren, childless woman.

Legions devoured her; idolaters took possession of her; they put the people Israel to the sword, and killed wantonly the faithful followers of the Most High.

Because of that Zion weeps bitterly; Jerusalem raises her voice.

24

How my heart grieves for the slain! How my heart yearns for the slain!

Jewish history. So many pogroms, expulsions, *autos-dafé,* then gas chambers, crematoria. Lands locked to refugees, locked to survivors. So many protests and memorial prayers.

Oh that my head were waters,
  and my eyes a fountain of tears,
that I might weep day and night
  for the slain of the daughter of my people!

Jeremiah 9:1

For two thousand years we have been a people in mourning. An extensive part of our poetry consists of *kinot,* lamentations. Yearning and sorrow fill most of our melodies. Yet, we are not alone in our grief.

Whenever Israel recites the *Kaddish* in the synagogues and proclaims, "May the great name be blessed forever and for all eternity," God's voice, we are told, responds, "Woe to that Father who has exiled His children, and woe to those children who have been exiled from their Father's hearth."

To the religious consciousness of the Jews the people being in exile meant also God's being in exile and the return of the people to the land is also experienced as God's return to the land. Three times a day we pray, "May our eyes behold Thy return and mercy to Zion." This is why we pray not only for the return of the people to Zion; we also pray that our eyes may *behold* the return of God to Zion.

For more than three thousand years we have been in love with Jerusalem. She occupied our hearts, filled our prayers, pervaded our dreams. Continually mourning her loss, our grief was not subdued when celebrating festivities, when arranging a dinner table, when painting our homes. No meal was concluded without imploring: "Build Jerusalem, speedily, in your own days. . . ." The two most solemn occasions of the year, the Seder on Passover, and the Day of Atonement, found their climax in the proclamation: "Next year in Jerusalem." And on the Sabbath we implored Him:

When will You reign in Zion?
Speedily, in our own days
Dwell there, and for ever!
May You be magnified and sanctified
In the midst of Jerusalem Thy city
Throughout all generations and to all eternity,
Let our eyes behold Thy kingdom. . . .

When a Jew arrived in the land, he bent and kissed the dust. When he saw the ruins he tore his garment. When placed in his grave, a handful of earth taken from the soil of the Holy Land was placed under his head.

> *Thus says the Lord:*
> *"A voice is heard in Ramah,*
> *lamentation and bitter weeping.*
> *Rachel is weeping for her children;*
> *she refuses to be comforted for her children,*
> *because they are not."*
> *Thus says the Lord:*
> *"Keep your voice from weeping,*
> *and your eyes from tears;*
> *for your work shall be rewarded, says the Lord,*
> *and they shall come back from the land of the*
> *enemy.*
> *There is hope for your future, says the Lord,*
> *and your children shall come back to their own*
> *country."*

Jeremiah 31:15–17

A CITY IN TRANCE

Jerusalem is a place to which we all turn when we pray, of which we all think when we hope, to which our hearts go to weep in common.

On the eve of the Sabbath, at the decisive moment, about to enter holiness in time, in the midst of calling upon the soul to welcome the Sabbath, we become engrossed in what is holy in space. What is holy in time has left its imprint on the land, on Jerusalem.

> *Sanctuary of the King, royal city, arise!*
> *Come forth from thy ruins.*
> *Long enough have you dwelt in the vale of tears.*

Here one feels: This city was meant to be by God.

There are hills in the world more impressive, valleys more blessed with fertility and beauty than those of the city of David. Yet none is so rich in allusions, so evocative.

Oblivion never enters here. Blasphemy, it seems, cannot be uttered here.

In Jerusalem there are houses, sewage, buses, lampposts. Yet she is more than a city among cities; she is a city full of vision, a city with an extrasensory dimension. Her fascination is not in her age. She is a dwelling place, not a collection of monuments, shrines. Her power is in her promise. Her very being is an earnest, a promise and a pledge.

Jerusalem has taken hold of me. I sit at the feet of the prophets and hear: "Sing and rejoice, O daughter of Zion, for lo, I come and I will dwell in the midst of you, says the Lord" (Zechariah 2:10).

Rejoice with Jerusalem, and be glad for her,
 all you who love her;
Rejoice with her in joy,
 all you who mourn over her.

Isaiah 66:10

Burning bush, invisibly burning. The heart is aflame, and faith is not consumed. Put off your shoes from your feet, get rid of pettiness. The hour is holy.

She is more than an area, a part of the land. She is a city in a state of trance. Here the prophets lived and ceased to live but their exaltation stayed on. Here the trees praise, the streets say grace, and my steps give thanks. The way of

29

Jerusalem is a way of exaltation. She is so much more than what you see.

Some experiences last a moment, others go on forever. We may not always experience the Shekinah, yet we can always mirror its meaning, be carried away by its thought.

Jerusalem, the charismatic city, is like a Hasidic master, whose sheer presence is a bestowal, whose heart and mind are never disengaged from God. The experience of the master's engagement to God enhances one's capacity for self-engagement to Him, and being present to Jerusalem opens gates.

Hatred contradicts the soul of man, distorts the air of Jerusalem; false steps defile the soil. Here we move along while the sky is gazing, soliciting, pleading.

Jerusalem is not the first among cities. She is the first among visions.

Jerusalem . . . Her excellence is in her being an event in the form of a city, the unfolding of the story concerning God and man. Her air is radiant with holiness in time, with meditations and reflections.

Jerusalem is more than pure possibility. Her distinction is in her election and charisma. Her holiness is in her being a place of meeting, for the present to meet the days to come, for the present never to be immune to intrusions of the past's moments, for days to commune with ages. Without Jerusalem the spiritual history of the world would be stagnant; with Jerusalem there is a vision and a promise.

What is the meaning of the name *Yerushalayim?* The city was first called *Shalom*—peace (Genesis 14:18), then Abraham named it *Yireh,* "whence the present saying, 'On the mount of the Lord there is vision' " (Genesis 22:14).

Yerushalayim combines both names: *Yireh* and *Shalom,* "vision" and "peace."

Jerusalem . . . Inundation of holiness in history, memory and assurance, hoary and close at hand, convergence of times, of times gone by and times to come, a suppressed resolve, a repressed outburst, and the imminence of redemption. Jerusalem is still, and occurs in a silent way.

When the Moors were driven out of Spain they left the land forever. When the Jews were driven out and no longer dwelled in the Holy Land, the land continued to dwell in them. This is the hymn of the exiles in Babylon.

By the waters of Babylon, there we sat down and wept,
when we remembered Zion.
On the willows there
we hung up our lyres.
For there our captors
required of us songs,
and our tormentors, mirth, saying,
"Sing us one of the songs of Zion!"

How shall we sing the Lord's song
in a foreign land?
If I forget you, O Jerusalem,

> *let my right hand wither!*
> *Let my tongue cleave to the roof of my mouth,*
>   *if I do not remember you,*
> *if I do not set Jerusalem*
>   *above my highest joy!*

> *Psalm 137:1–6*

Jerusalem on earth continued as Jerusalem in the souls. Her stones became moments, space became time. The Jewish people has never ceased to be passionate about Jerusalem.

The eyes of history are upon the city of David, upon "the faithful city." Its authenticity cannot be borrowed. Oxford, Paris, Tanglewood, for all the beauty and learning emanating from them, cannot serve as models for shaping the way, the role, and the image of Jerusalem.

There is no joy without Jerusalem, and there is no perception of Jerusalem without the perception of her mystery.

What is the mystery of Jerusalem? A promise: peace and God's presence.

First there was a vision: God's vision of human being. Then He created man according to His vision, according to His image. But man's resemblance to God's image is fading rapidly.

God had a vision of restoring the image of man. So He created a city in heaven and called it Jerusalem, hoping and praying that Jerusalem on earth may resemble Jerusalem in heaven.

Jerusalem is a recalling, an insisting and a waiting for the answer to God's hope.

THE CHALLENGE

The mystery that is Jerusalem, the challenge that is Jerusalem! How to unite the human and the holy? How to echo the divine in the shape of words, in the form of deeds?

Now that we are at home in the city of David, what is required of us? What message does this new chapter in Jewish history hold in store?

How shall we live with Jerusalem? She is a queen demanding high standards. What does she expect of us, living in an age of spiritual obtuseness, near exhaustion? What sort of light should glow in Zion? What words, what thoughts, what vision should come out of Zion?

33

The challenge is staggering. Let us pray that we may not fail. Let us prepare the minds and the hearts for the vision of Isaiah concerning Judaism and Jerusalem.

> *It shall come to pass in the latter days*
> *that the mountain of the house of the Lord*
> *shall be established as the highest of the mountains,*
> *and shall be raised above the hills;*
> *and all the nations shall flow to it,*
> *and many peoples shall come, and say:*
> *"Come, let us go up to the mountain of the Lord,*
> *to the house of the God of Jacob;*
> *that he may teach us his ways*
> *and that we may walk in his paths."*
> *For out of Zion shall go forth the law,*
> *and the word of the Lord from Jerusalem.*
> *He shall judge between the nations,*
> *and shall decide for many peoples;*
> *and they shall beat their swords into plowshares,*
> *and their spears into pruning hooks;*
> *nation shall not lift up sword against nation,*
> *neither shall they learn war any more.*

> *Isaiah 2:2–4*

We must beware lest the place of David becomes a commonplace.

One is terribly apprehensive. How do you live in the city of God? How do you match the infinitely holy with justice

and compassion, with song and prayer? How do you live in
a sanctuary day and night?

> *Who shall ascend the hill of the Lord?*
> *And who shall stand in his holy place?*
> *He who has clean hands and a pure heart,*
> *who does not lift up his soul to what is false,*
> *and does not swear deceitfully.*

Psalm 24:3–4

> *O Lord, who shall sojourn in thy tent?*
> *Who shall dwell on thy holy hill?*
> *He who walks blamelessly, and does what is right,*
> *and speaks truth from his heart;*
> *who does not slander with his tongue,*
> *and does no evil to his friend,*
> *nor takes up a reproach against his neighbor;*
> *in whose eyes a reprobate is despised,*
> *but who honors those who fear the Lord;*
> *who swears to his own hurt and does not change;*
> *who does not put out his money at interest,*
> *and does not take a bribe against the innocent.*
> *He who does these things shall never be moved.*

Psalm 15

What should come out of Zion? Renunciation of lies,
compassion, disgust with violence, helps to overcome the
infirmity of the spirit.

Jerusalem is more than a place in space or a memorial to glories of the past. Jerusalem is a prelude, anticipation of days to come.

"At that time Jerusalem shall be called the throne of the Lord, and all nations shall gather to it, to the presence of the Lord in Jerusalem, and they shall no more stubbornly follow their own evil heart" (Jeremiah 3:17).

How to prepare the city for such destiny? How to qualify for such calling?

It is one of the great marvels of history that Jerusalem is sacred not only to the Jews but also to Christians and to Moslems all over the world.

King Solomon in inaugurating the Temple at Jerusalem prayed: "Likewise when a foreigner, who is not of thy people Israel, comes from a far country for thy name's sake (for they shall hear of thy great name, and thy mighty hand, and of thy outstretched arm), when he comes and prays toward this house, hear thou in heaven thy dwelling place, and do according to all for which the foreigner calls to thee; in order that all the peoples of the earth may know thy name and fear thee, as do thy people Israel, and that they may know that this house which I have built is called by thy name" (I Kings 8:41–43).

Who will fan and force the fire of truth to spread across the world, insisting that we are all one, that mankind is not an animal species but a fellowship of care, a covenant of brotherhood?

None shall fear, none shall hurt.

There is cursing in the world, scheming, and very little praying. Let Jerusalem inspire praying: an end to rage, an end to violence.

Let Jerusalem be a seat of mercy for all men. Wherever a sigh is uttered, it will evoke active compassion in Jerusalem.

Let there be no waste of history. This must be instilled in those who might be walking in the streets of Jerusalem like God's butlers in the sacred palace. Here no one is more than a guest.

Jerusalem must not be lost to pride or to vanity.

All of Jerusalem is a gate, but the key is lost in the darkness of God's silence. Let us light all the lights, let us call all the names, to find the key.

Thus says the Lord: I will return to Zion and will dwell in the midst of Jerusalem, and Jerusalem shall be called the faithful city and the mountain of the Lord of hosts, the holy mountain (Zechariah 8:3).

Your eyes will see Jerusalem,
   a quiet habitation, an immovable tent,
whose stakes will never be plucked up,
   nor will any of its cords be broken.
But there the Lord in majesty will be for us . . . .

Isaiah 33:20–21

At that time Jerusalem shall be called the throne of the Lord, and all nations shall gather to it, to the presence of the Lord in Jerusalem . . . (Jeremiah 3:17).

For my house shall be a house of prayer
for all peoples

Isaiah 56:7

2
Engagement
to the land

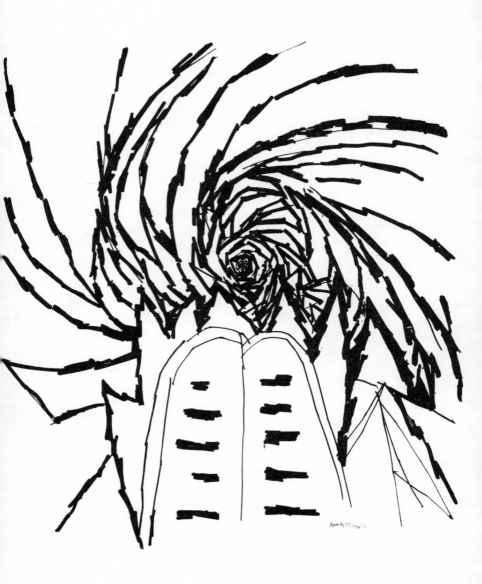

TO REPUDIATE THE BIBLE?

Unprecedented. A people despised, persecuted, scattered to all corners of the earth, has the audacity to dream of regaining authenticity, of being free in the Holy Land.

For nearly two thousand years and many times a day in joy and sorrow we prayed for you, Jerusalem, and our prayers never turned pale. What is it we implore the Lord every Sabbath as we are about to open the Ark to take out the Torah?

Merciful Father,
Deal kindly with Zion,
Rebuild the walls of Jerusalem.

43

Truly, in Thee alone we trust
High and exalted King and God, eternal God.

Despoiled and dispersed, abased and harassed, we knew we were not estranged forever. We mourned you, we never wept you away. Hope was hatched in the nests of agony.

The love of this land was due to an imperative, not to an instinct, not to a sentiment. There is a covenant, an engagement of the people to the land. We live by covenants. We could not betray our pledge or discard the promise.

When Israel was driven into exile, the pledge became a prayer; the prayer a dream; the dream a passion, a duty, a dedication.

Intimate attachment to the land, waiting for the renewal of Jewish life in the land of Israel, is part of our integrity, an existential fact. Unique, *sui generis,* it lives in our hopes, it abides in our hearts.

It is a commitment we must not betray. Three thousand years of faithfulness cannot be wiped off.

To abandon the land would make a mockery of all our longings, prayers, and commitments. To abandon the land would be to repudiate the Bible.

THE BIBLE IS OUR DESTINY

What is unique about Jewish existence? The fact that ours is not a free association with the Bible. We are her offspring, her outcome. Her spirit is our destiny. What is our destiny? To be a community in whom the Bible lives on.

We are close to the biblical people, to those who were both commanded and reprimanded, to those who were slaves in Egypt, to those who stood at the foot of Sinai. We continue to be the stunned contemporaries of the prophets.

"Ye are my witnesses, says the Lord, and I am God" (Isaiah 43:12). A rabbi of the second century took the statement to mean, if you are my witnesses, I am God; if you cease to be my witnesses, I am not God. This is one of the boldest utterances in Jewish literature, a manifesto of meaning. If there are no witnesses, there is no God to be met. There is a mystery, an enigma, a darkness past finding out. For God to be present there must be witnesses. Without the people Israel, the Bible is mere literature. Through Israel, the Bible is a voice, a power and a challenge.

45

Far from being a mere relic of ancient literature, a book on the shelf gathering dust, the Bible in our lives is living power, radiating anticipations, throwing illuminations.

Not a document sealed and finished. It is a book alive, a book that goes on and extends into the present—always being written, always disclosing and unfolding. We are in labor with biblical visions.

The Bible is essentially the history of the Covenant of God and Israel, the story of God in search of man through the mutual commitment of God and Israel. The Bible lives on because the Covenant endures. The central theme of the story of the Covenant is the promise of the land to Abraham.

The Bible is not an end but a beginning; a precedent, not a story—the perennial motion of the spirit. It is a book that cannot die, that is incapable of becoming stale or obsolete. Oblivion shuns its pages. Its power is not subsiding. In fact, it is still at the very beginning of its career, the full meaning of its content having hardly touched the threshold of our minds; like an ocean at the bottom of which countless pearls lie; waiting to be discovered, its spirit is still to be unfolded. Though its words seem plain and its idiom translucent, unnoticed meanings, undreamed-of intimations break forth constantly. More than two thousand years of reading and research have not succeeded in exploring its full meaning. Today it is as if it had never been touched, never been seen, as if we had not even begun to read it. What would be missing in the world, what would be the condition and faith of man, had the Bible not been preserved?

THE ECLIPSE OF THE BIBLE

An ominous development is taking place in the twentieth century: man's increasing failure or inability to take the Bible seriously, his growing alienation from the Bible. Its grandeur is becoming inaccessible, a preserve of the past, not a perspective of the present. Its challenge vanishing from our thinking, from our convictions, it survives for illustration, for edification, remaining outside our imagination or our decisions in shaping thoughts, deeds.

Jean Jacques Rousseau, the first to recognize that the modern venture was a radical error, sought the remedy in a return to classical thought. The movement of Jewish re-

47

newal having recognized the tragic plight of the Jewish people, sought the remedy in a return to the land and the language of the Bible.

God has a vision. The Bible is an interpretation of the vision. God has a dream. The task of Israel is to interpret the dream.

Western civilization is in a profound way mankind's confrontation with the Bible. Its intellectual development, its moral views, have been shaped by the continuous impact of Scripture. That impact is subsiding. We witness a radical elimination of the Bible from the life of the people in many parts of the world.

We of this generation stand face to face with events of vast magnitude. The Lord of history does neither slumber nor sleep.

As a people we do not set our own goals, and are frequently mistaken in our self-understanding. We live by a promise. That promise appeared and reappeared in our souls, in our faith, a never muted voice. It renews itself now as a command.

The path to Palestine was paved with prophetic words. In the upbuilding of the land we are aware of responding to the biblical Covenant, to an imperative that kept on speaking to us throughout the ages, and which never became obsolete or stale. A tree rooted in the Bible will never wither.

It was particularly during the awesome days of May and

June of 1967 that a new certainty emerged. The Bible, we discovered, is not a book sealed and completed; the Bible lives on, always being written, continuously proclaimed. The Bible, we discovered, lives within us, reverberates in our anxiety. Our involvement with it continues. Almost suddenly it dawned upon many of us that biblical history is alive, that chapters of the Bible are being written.

It is a renaissance of biblical events that we witness in our days.

SINGULARITY

Israel reborn represents a breakthrough into whole new areas of experience and understanding. It defies conventional conceptions, ordinary expectations. Its essence is a proclamation.

This is why the return to Zion is a source of embarrassment to so many of us who depend for intellectual efficacy

upon conformity with mental habits. In our scientific inves-
tigations, we use conceptual models in order to characterize
an empirical situation under investigation; we are guided
by the principle of generalization, seeking to fit a particular object to a universal model. The relation between model
and things modeled is a relation of analogy.

In other words, our mental habit is to think in terms of
sameness and to assume that things under consideration are
mere copies, repetitions, and to disregard the unprecedented, distinctness, uniqueness. We operate with established forms, with rubrics.

This is indeed the modern religious predicament. The
mysterious events so central to Judaism and Christianity
seem so strange because they are unprecedented.

The return to Zion is an unprecedented drama, an event
sui generis for which there is no model, no analogy.

The State of Israel is a surprise, yet the modern mind
hates to be surprised. Never before has a nation been restored to its ancient hearth after a lapse of 1,897 years.
This extraordinary aspect is bound to carry some shock to
the conventional mind, to be a scandal to the mediocre
mind and a foolishness to the positivists. It requires reorder-
ing of some notions.

Here lies a lesson of importance. It is the homogeniza-
tion of history that often deprives us of understanding.

Genuine history is not mere repetition, moving in a
circle. It is a fresh attempt, a new arrival. The Bible begins

with the words "At the beginning . . . ." To Greek mythology, for example, where the assumption is that the world has always been in existence, the concept of beginning was inconceivable. Jewish understanding further implies that also in history there can be novelty, beginning.

Israel is a miracle in disguise. Things look natural and conceal what is a radical surprise. Zion rebuilt becomes a harbinger of a new understanding, of how history is intertwined with the mystery.

Israel is the opposite of a commonplace, it is an extraordinary place, and it is on the verge of the extraordinary that we may encounter the marvel. Israel as a novelty is not an absolutely new beginning, but a resurrection in Ezekiel's sense. It is an accord of a divine promise and a human achievement.

51

THE DRAMA

The theme is not an idea but a story, a drama. The *dramatis personae:* a people, a land, and a divine presence. The drama has many scenes.

First comes the election of one man whose vocation is to proclaim the sovereignty of the One, demanding justice and supreme sacrifice, and who is to be a father of many nations and a blessing to all nations. His vocation is to be continued by his seed, a people yet to be born, a people to be given a home, a land. But before inheriting the land they must go through the agony of slavery, through redemption and the trials of forty years in the wilderness.

After centuries of battles and tribulations the people inherit the Promised Land. David is king, Jerusalem the capital, and the Temple is built.

To the neighbors, and later to some Hebrew rulers themselves, the commonwealth of David is a state like other states. There are wars, jealousy, idolatry, and corruption. It is an open land, the only fortification is the sacred Covenant and faithfulness to it. The crisis comes, it is followed by disaster. Jerusalem destroyed, the people driven into exile.

Destruction and exile are commonplace in the ancient Near East. It happened to many peoples: their culture obliterated, their identity lost, they sink into oblivion. The land is occupied by others.

In sharp contrast, the unprecedented happened. The Jewish people refuse to abandon the Covenant and their love of Jerusalem, their attachment to the land. Empires come and go. After seventy years, Cyrus makes it possible for them to return to the land.

The story is known. Other people had meanwhile occupied their country, and some time later pagan rulers sought to dominate the religious and cultural life in the land. Here we must pause and ponder. Had Ezra and Nehemiah failed, had the Samaritans prevailed, had the Maccabeans been defeated, what would have been the spiritual fate of the world?

In the whirlwind of history the Bible would have been forgotten, there would have been neither Judaism nor Christianity nor Islam; Abraham, Moses, Isaiah would be only vague memories.

It happened again. In the year 70 Jerusalem was destroyed, the people driven into exile or sold into slavery. Yet Jews clung to the land.

53

CONTINUOUSLY ASSERTING OUR RIGHT

The restoration of Zion began on the day of its destruction. The land was rebuilt in time long before it was restored in space. We have been building it daily for nearly two thousand years.

In the blessings of grace we say, "Blessed be Thou who is building Jerusalem, Amen." We never said "Who will build." He *is* building Jerusalem.

If one takes an article by violence and the owner does not abandon hope of regaining it, neither can consecrate it (give it to the sanctuary): the one, because it is not his; the other, because it is not actually in his possession.[1] The land was taken from the Jewish people by violence, and we have never abandoned hope of regaining it.

Throughout the ages we said No to all the conquerors of Palestine. We said No before God and man emphatically,

[1] Kiddushin, 52b; Rabbi J. J. Reines, see *Sefer Hamizrahi* (Jerusalem, 1946), p. 10.

daily. We objected to their occupations, we rejected their claims, we deepened our attachment, knowing that the occupation by the conquerors was a passing adventure, while our attachment to the land was an eternal link.

The Jewish people has never ceased to assert its right, its title, to the land of Israel. This continuous, uninterrupted insistence, an intimate ingredient of Jewish consciousness, is at the core of Jewish history, a vital element of Jewish faith.

How did the Jews contest and call into question the occupation of the land by the mighty empires of East and West? How did they assert their own title to the land?

Our protest was not heard in the public squares of the large cities. It was uttered in our homes, in our sanctuaries, in our books, in our prayers. Indeed, our very existence as a people was a proclamation of our link to the land, of our certainty of return.

It may sound quite plausible to argue that if the right of the Jews to return to Palestine is admitted on the grounds of history, then the whole map of the world would have to be remade and chaos would ensue. But does the question really arise? Do the descendants of the Romans, for example, claim entry into England? Do they need England? Does their future, their very existence, depend on settling there? Or do Arabs, for that matter, press to return to Andalusia in Spain? Is it a matter of life and death for them? The analogy is fallacious and misleading.

55

There is no such attachment to a land anywhere else in the world.

The Second Commonwealth was destroyed by the Romans in the year 70, the State of Israel was born in the year 1948.

In that long interval, Palestine never became a national home for any other people, has never been regarded as a geopolitical entity, has never been an independent state. It was conquered and reconquered no less than fourteen times in thirteen centuries. Each conquest absorbed it as occupied territory to be ruled from without. And each left its legacy in the form of soldiers and slaves and their descendants, sharing no ethnic or cultural identity, and constrained during the Arab conquest to accept Islam as a creed or be put to affliction. Universal was the legacy of desolation. Most of the country had sunk back into the oblivion of swamp in the north and eroded soil and sand in the south. The nineteenth century found in the land a veritable hodge-podge of nations, ethnic and linguistic groups, and religious beliefs. Except for the Jews, none regarded Palestine as a homeland, as a national political unit worthy of independence and nationhood. To the Turks, it was simply a remote province of the Ottoman empire; to some Arabs, a small segment which might be annexed to a greater Arab empire, or enhance this or that dynastic dream of expansionism, if such there were to be;

for others it might merely have religious and diverse associations and sentiments. For the Jews, and for them alone, this was the one and only Homeland, the only conceivable place where they could find liberation and independence, the land toward which their minds and hearts had been uplifted for a score of centuries and where their roots had clung in spite of all adversity. For the Jewish national movement, therefore, the land of Israel was not merely a place where, historically speaking, the Jews had once dwelt. It was the homeland with which an indestructible bond of national, physical, religious, and spiritual character had been preserved, and where the Jews had in essence remained—and were now once more in fact—a major element of the population. Whatever greatness came about in this land—in song, in story, in human personalities, in ideas, in inspiration—was the result of Jewish living in the land.

It is here where the great works of the Jewish people came into being: the Bible, the Mishnah, the Palestinian Talmud, the Midrashim, the Shulhan Arukh, Lurianic mysticism. No other people has created original literary works of decisive significance in the land of Israel.

The words, the songs, the chants of Jewish liturgy, which have shaped the life of prayer in both Judaism and Christianity, were *born* in the Holy Land.

It was in this land that a man of Israel, the son of an

Israelite carpenter, proclaimed the gospel of love to the pagan world and cleared the way for the days of the Messiah.

The great Arab contributions came from Mecca, Cairo, Damascus, Baghdad, not from Jerusalem. To the Arab nations Erets Israel (Land of Israel) is two percent of a vast territory they inhabit; to the Jewish people Erets Israel is home, hope, and all they can call their own.

It is not only memory, our past, that ties us to the land; it is our hope, our future.

IN DIALOGUE WITH THE LAND

Throughout history people have moved from one country to another, voluntarily or involuntarily. Finding a new land, they abandoned the memory of their former homes. The Jewish people, however, forced to leave their ancient country, has never abandoned, has never forsaken the Holy Land; the Jewish people has never ceased to be passionate about Zion. It has always lived in a dialogue with the Holy Land.

Exile from the land was conceived as an interruption, as a prelude to return, never as an abandonment or detachment. Bonds of hope tied us to the land. To abandon these bonds was to deny our identity. Again and again our hearts turned to Zion and Jerusalem as the needle to the pole, as the dial to the sun.

After the collapse of the Bar Kochba rebellion, when Jews were no longer permitted to be at home in their own land, Zion—Jerusalem—did not simply linger on as a vague memory of a distant past. Zion, Jerusalem, continued to be a presence in our lives. Wherever we lived, the sky was above us, and the thought of Jerusalem in the front of us.

The destruction of Jerusalem in the year 70, the onset of a history of distress, remained a lasting sorrow and hurt. Throughout the ages it was as if since the year 70 time stood still. All calamities were seen as a sequel to the destruction of Jerusalem. The disaster was constantly lived and relived, the anguish never ceased.

It was experienced as a cosmic disaster, affecting the lives of all men. "Since the Temple was destroyed the world has not witnessed the true radiance of the sun."

59

Separation from the land was never accepted as final. The vision of restoration, craving for redemption, love of Zion, longing for Jerusalem, fill the words of our liturgy, words that give no rest.

MEMORY

Why did our hearts and minds throughout the ages turn to Erets Israel, to the Holy Land? Because of memory, because of hope, because of distress.

Because of memory. There is a slow and silent stream, a stream not of oblivion but of memory, from which we must constantly drink before entering the realm of faith. To believe is to remember. The substance of our very being is memory, our way of living is retaining the reminders, articulating memory.[2]

2 See Abraham J. Heschel, *Man Is Not Alone* (New York: Farrar, Straus, 1951), pp. 161 ff. According to Jewish mysticism, forgetting

Jewish memory, far from turning into a collection of stale reminiscences, was kept alive by the power of hope and imagination, transcending the limits of believing. What seemed unbelievable became a foregone conclusion.

After the destruction of Jerusalem, the city did not simply become a vague memory of the distant past; it continued to live as an inspiration in the hearts and minds of the people.

Jerusalem became a central hope, symbol of all hopes. It became the recurring theme of our liturgy. Thus even when the minds were not aware of it, the words reminded us, the words cried for restoration of Zion and intensified the link, the attachment.

Yehudah Halevi, the famed Jewish poet of the eleventh century, expresses this feeling in the following lines:

> *Would that I have wings that I could wend my way to Thee, O Jerusalem, from afar!*
> *I will make my own broken heart find its way amidst your broken ruins.*
> *I will fall upon my face to the ground, for I take much delight in your stones and show favor to your very dust.*
> *The air of your land is the very life of our soul.*

---

comes from the realm of evil and the unclean. Had the Tablets containing the Ten Commandments not been broken, there would have been no forgetting. See Zohar, I, 193b.

61

When Jerusalem was destroyed, the sages decreed that each person make remembrance of Jerusalem every day in every place. Thus they said, "A person shall lime the walls of his home, but leave a corner untouched. . . . A person shall traverse all the courses of a repast, and leave some morsel untouched. . . . A woman shall make her jewelry and make some part incomplete, for it is said, 'If I forget you, O Jerusalem.' "

Numerous rituals are performed in remembrance of the destruction—*zecher lehurban*. Three weeks of sorrow, particularly nine days of mourning, are part of our liturgical year. The "three weeks" end on the ninth day of the Hebrew month of Av, which is a fast of twenty-four hours, observed year after year in recollecting the destruction of the land and the people. People assemble in the synagogues, take off their shoes; they sit with bowed heads on the floor, crying for the land, reciting the Book of Lamentations.

In joy and in grief Zion is never absent from our thoughts. The liturgical words of comfort which are said to people in mourning are: "May the Lord comfort you among all those that mourn for Zion and Jerusalem." Even to this day, at the conclusion of the joyous ritual of a wedding, a glass is broken in remembrance of the destruction of Jerusalem. In the benedictions that solemnize the wedding, a prayer is said for the joy of Jerusalem.

May Zion rejoice
as her children are restored to her in joy.

Praised be Thou, O Lord,
who causes Zion to rejoice at her children's
* return. . . .*
Praised be Thou, O Lord our God,
King of the universe,
who created joy and gladness,
bride and groom,
mirth, song, delight and rejoicing,
love, brotherhood, peace and fellowship.
O Lord our God,
May there soon be heard
in the cities of Judah
and in the streets of Jerusalem,
the voice of joy and gladness,
the voice of bride and groom,
the jubilant voice of those
joined in marriage under their bridal canopy,
the voice of young people
feasting and singing. . . .

When the newborn is received into the community a blessing is pronounced that "he may become worthy to ascend in the holy pilgrimage of the three festivals," and, as we have mentioned before, when the dead is laid to rest a small sack of earth from the Holy Land is placed under his head. In life and in death we have never parted from the Holy Land. At the conclusion of each meal, reciting grace, we say, "Take pity O Lord our God on Israel Thy people, on Jerusalem Thy city, on Mount Zion the habitation of

Thy glory. . . . Build Jerusalem, the Holy City, speedily, in our own days. . . ." In the penitential liturgy we pray, "Remember Mount Zion, remember, O Lord, the affection of Jerusalem, never forget the love of Zion; Thou wilt arise and have pity on Zion; for it is time to favor her, for the appointed time has come."

For these many ages, in many lands, whether in Spain or in India, in Egypt or in Poland, no day, no evening passes without praying for Zion and Jerusalem. We pray for her recovery, we pray for her redemption, for her prosperity and for her peace.

Three times every day, wherever on earth he stood, whatever his anguish, every Jew entreated his Maker: "Have mercy, O Lord, and return to Jerusalem, Thy city." And again: "May our eyes behold Thy return in mercy to Zion." At festivals, a few pray: "May it be Thy Will, O Lord our God and God of our fathers, that Thou again have mercy upon us. . . . Bring us to Zion, Thy city, with song, to Jerusalem, the site of Thy sanctuary, with everlasting joy. . . ."

Attachment to the land of Israel so dominates our liturgy that the prayers for dew and for rain accord with the seasons of the Holy Land rather than with the climates of the lands in which the worshipers recite the prayers.

"At midnight I rise to praise Thee" (Psalm 119:62), said King David. The evening is a time for study, midnight is a time for song and praise.

64

A harp was hung over David's bed and at midnight the north wind would blow and it would play by itself. Then the king was constrained to rise from his bed, and till the dawn flushed the eastern skies, he would break out into song and praise.[3]

The music was not silenced with the disappearance of the harp of David. It kept awake many pious Jews even during the Middle Ages. Throughout ten centuries there were those who would rise at midnight every night, except Friday night, put on clothes of mourning, cover the head with ashes, sit on the floor, recite prayers expressing grief over the destruction of the Temple and the suffering of God's children in the dispersion. A whole liturgy developed for this service, part of which was a confession of sins that are the cause of deferring the manifestation of the glory of God and the establishing of the kingship of God on earth.[4]

This service, observed in many lands by mystics, by Hasidim, as well as by simple people in the stillness of the night, in the privacy of their homes, ended on a note of certainty that God's glory will prevail.

Sermons were preached in the synagogues and houses of study about the sanctity of the land, and even sermons which did not deal with this theme would frequently con-

---

[3] Berachoth 3b; Midrash Tehillim 22.8; see Yerushalmi, Berachoth 3d.
[4] See S. Schechter, *Studies in Judaism* (Philadelphia, 1908), second series, pp. 205 f.

clude with the words "and a redeemer shall come into Zion. Amen."

History seems to present to us the depressing spectacle of a bewildering variety of thoughts and beliefs and, above all, of the passing away of every thought and belief ever held by men, of vanishing loyalties, of unabashed betrayals. The loyalty of the Jewish people to the promise is itself an anchor of meaning.

Any attempt to impair the vital link between Israel the people and Israel the land is an affront to biblical faith. The horrendous sin of the children of Israel in the wilderness was the worship of the Golden Calf—yet that sin was forgiven. However, when, under the influence of those who were sent by Moses to scout out the land and who upon return spread calumnies about the land, the Israelites lost their faith in ever entering the land—that sin was not forgiven (Numbers 14:29 ff.). For the spies who spread slander about the land were not forgiven. For the sin of the spies and the acceptance of the slander by the people, the entire generation which left Egypt died in the wilderness. The Blessed Holy One could forgo His own honor, but could not forgive the transgression in slandering the Promised Land.

What we have witnessed in our own days is a reminder of the power of God's mysterious promise to Abraham and a testimony to the fact that the people kept its pledge, "If I

66

forget you, O Jerusalem, let my right hand wither" (Psalm 137:5). The Jew in whose heart the love of Zion dies is doomed to lose his faith in the God of Abraham, who gave the land as an earnest of the redemption of all men.

We have never abandoned the land, and it is as if the land has never abandoned the Jewish people. Attempts to establish other civilizations in the land ended in failure. Numerous conquerors invaded the land; Romans, Byzantines, Arabs, Kurds, Mongols, Mamelukes, Tartars, and Turks. But what did these people make of the land? No one built the state or shaped a nation.

The land did not respond.

DWELLING IN THE LAND

From the time of Joshua to this day, for a period of more than 3,300 years, Jews have lived in the land of Israel in unbroken sequence. After the destruction of Jerusalem by

67

the Babylonians in the year 586 B.C.E., and again after the destruction of the Second Commonwealth by the Romans, in the year 70, Jews continued to dwell in the land.

Though the major part of the nation was forced into exile, there has always remained a Jewish settlement in Palestine. Its fortunes varied from generation to generation, but its continuity was never broken. However terrible the oppression, the Jews never abandoned their native land. Nor did they merge into any of the numerous racial and religious communities which held sway in Palestine in subsequent centuries. They remained a distinctive national-religious entity, temporarily subjugated, but never doubtful of their ultimate restoration.

They clung to their native soil with fierce tenacity, as evidenced by the literature and the historical monuments of their conquerors. They never resigned themselves to their exile, as did so many other conquered nations of antiquity. When they were released from the Babylonian captivity, it was Jewish noblemen and high officials in the Persian service who headed the returning exiles. They fought with unparalleled courage and resource against the imperial power of Rome. The last phase of the second Jewish state was an almost uninterrupted series of revolts against the Roman provincial governors. The final revolt, known as the Judaean War, was, according to Roman records, one of the fiercest national struggles which the Roman legions ever had to face. Even after the conquest of

Jerusalem and the destruction of their national sanctuary, they did not give up the struggle for their independence.

Fifty years later they rose again in a great national insurrection and for many months defied the Roman forces until at last they were crushed. It was as the result of that devastating defeat that the Jewish political power in Palestine was finally destroyed. Yet for centuries after that destruction the Jews continued to cling stubbornly to the country, and it was only the policy of extermination and expropriation pursued by the Romans and Byzantines which in the end drove the bulk of the Jewish people out of Palestine.

At the time of the first crusades, e.g., there still existed fair-sized agricultural Jewish populations, especially in Galilee. There were important Jewish communities in Jerusalem, Acre, Haifa, Jaffa, Ashkelon, Ramlah, and Gaza.

In the perspective of persecution and oppression during the time of the crusades, a wave of Messianic yearning swept the Jewish communities in many lands. In the Holy Land there was a movement of the Mourners for Zion, which for generations had attracted waves of immigrants from all parts of the Diaspora.

Benjamin of Tudela, the famous Jewish traveler of the twelfth century, offered the following description of the adherents of the movement: "They eat no bread and drink no wine. They are dressed in black garments and live in caves. They fast all their lives and on the Sabbath and the

Holy Days, and pray incessantly for the return of the exiled sons of Israel."[5]

Despite the persecutions brought about by the crusaders and subsequent invasions of the Tartars, some Jewish settlements continued in the ancient homeland, including a handful of agricultural settlements in Upper Galilee, where Jews have lived from the days of the second Temple until this day.

Return to Zion is more than a phenomenon of our time. As a hope, as a dream, as an article of faith, it lived in the hearts of the Jews of all ages. Indeed, there never was a time in which the Holy Land was not an object of attraction and deep longing for the pious Jew, even though he was not always able to gratify his longing. There was an awareness in many minds that life was incomplete, that one's service was deficient, unless one lived in the Holy Land.

1492 . . . The expulsion of the Jews from Spain. Many exiles turned their eyes to the land of their fathers. The journey to the land was perilous, life in the land hazardous. Yet many exiles, convinced that their recent tribulations were a prelude to "the pangs of the Messiah," a prelude to the coming of the Messianic redemption, settled in the Holy Land. Palestine became a great center of rab-

[5] *The Itinerary of Benjamin of Tudela*, translated by M. A. Adler (London, 1907), p. 48.

binic learning and spiritual life. The newcomers, some of whom brought technical skills and experience in trade, brought about an economic revitalization of the land. The city of Safed in Galilee became the seat of great saints, scholars, and mystics.

In the sixteenth century, Joseph, the Duke of Naxos, inspired by his aunt, Doña Gracia Nasi, seemed to have realized the necessity of finding not a temporary haven of refuge for the Jews, but a permanent one. There was only one safe place for persecuted Jewry: Palestine. He intended to make Tiberias in Galilee a Jewish center.[6] With astonishing tenacity, the original Jewish settlement managed to survive through a long succession of invasions and catastrophes until late in the Middle Ages. In the mountain village of Pekiin in Galilee a flawless line of descent can be traced from the Hebrews of yore to the present-day inhabitants. To live in the atmosphere of the Holy Land was a dream of the pious, and there were always individuals who defied all obstacles and went to settle there. Many followed the example of Jacob and requested to be buried in the Holy Land, while others settled there in their old age. Whoever left his home town for Israel earned the deep respect of his friends and neighbors.

Until recent times the journey to the Holy Land was

[6] Cecil Roth, *House of Nasi: The Duke of Naxos* (Philadelphia: Jewish Publication Society, 1948), p. 195.

71

fraught with hardship and danger. Travelers would spend many years journeying in rickety carts, on ill-paved roads, and in unseaworthy sailing craft. Many people would leave their homes and property, their families and friends, to wander from country to country in an attempt to reach the Holy Land. They were often exposed to persecution and mockery, an easy prey to robbers and cut-throats. Yet they willingly risked all these privations to accomplish their desire, and for the many who perished on the way the Holy Land was their dying thought. Those who were fortunate enough to reach their destination arrived, for the most part, utterly destitute. They lived in great poverty and frequently in fear of their very lives, for conditions in the land were most insecure. It was only because of their great love for the country, because of their conviction that "the merit of living in the land of Israel equals the merit of observing all the commandments of the Torah" and hastens the redemption of the land and the people, that they were able to hold out. They accepted the tribulations bound up with life in Palestine in those days with love; and it was they who paved the way for the pioneers of the national revival in modern times.

What arriving and dwelling in the land meant to Jewish tradition is reflected in the following sober words of the Code of Maimonides.

The greatest of our sages used to kiss (the rocks) on the borders of Palestine. They used to kiss the stones of the land and roll themselves in its dust, as it is written: For thy servants take pleasure in her stones, and love her dust (Ps. 102:15).

The rabbis said that the sins of him who lives in Palestine are forgiven, as it is written: and the inhabitant shall not say: "I am sick"; the people that dwell therein shall be forgiven their iniquity (Isa. 33:24). Even if one walks four cubits in it, one is assured of life in the world to come. So too, one who is buried there will obtain atonement: It is as though the place (where one lies) were an altar which effects atonement, as it is said: And the land doth make expiation for his people (Deut. 32:43). In (forecasting) punishment (the Prophet) says: And thou thyself shalt die in an unclean land (Amos 7:17). There is no comparison between one whom Palestine receives while he is living and one whom it receives after his death: Nevertheless the greatest among our wise men brought their dead there. Think of Jacob, our Father, and of Joseph, the Righteous!

At all times one should live in Palestine even in a place the majority of whose population is heathen, and not live outside Palestine even in a place the majority of whose population is Jewish; for he who leaves Palestine is as though he would serve idolatry, as it is written: For they have driven me out this day that I should not cleave unto the inheritance of the Lord, saying: Go, serve other Gods (I Sam. 26:19). In (predicting) punishment, the Prophet says: Neither shall they enter into the land of Israel (Ezek. 13:9).[7]

---

[7] *The Code of Maimonides*, Book XIV, The Book of Judges, Kings, ch. 5, 10 ff. (Yale Judaica Series, Vol. III).

For centuries after the destruction of the Holy Temple, every year during the Feast of Tabernacles there were large meetings on the Mount of Olives constituted of pilgrims from Palestine itself, Babylon, Egypt, and perhaps also from Europe.

The longing for Zion, the persecutions, and the long wait for redemption gave rise from time to time to Messianic movements, led by individuals who claimed to be divinely appointed to bring about the establishment of the Messianic kingdom. Some of these pseudo-Messiahs were impostors, others were sincere. Most of them sought to accomplish the return of the Jewish people to its native land through penitence and prayer.

There had, indeed, been a continuous chain of Messianic waves ever since, and in fact even prior to, the destruction of the Jewish state. Moses of Crete in the fifth century, Serenus of Syria and Abu Isa of Ispahan in the eighth, David Alroy of Baghdad in the twelfth, Abulafia of Messina in the thirteenth, Asher Lemmlein of Istria at the end of the fifteenth, David Reubeni and Solomon Molcho in the sixteenth, all these pseudo-Messiahs of succeeding ages indicate the ever-present readiness of the Jewish masses throughout the Diaspora to abandon at a moment's notice what they considered as their merely temporary homes, relinquish their worldly possessions and embark on the precarious journey to the land of their destiny. The leaders might be genuine mystics or ambitious impostors, the call for the return to Zion was as irresistible in the sixteenth century as it had been in the fifth. In the wake of the overwhelming tragedy of the expulsion of the Jews from Spain and of the fearful massacres in the Ukraine in the following century, the Messianic longing assumed an unprecedented intensity. It reached its apogee in the movement led by Sabbatai Zevi who, in the middle of the seventeenth century, proclaimed himself Messiah and produced a spiritual upheaval such as had never before shaken the Diaspora. Active preparations were set on foot in all parts of the Jewish world. The Messianic ecstasy found its adherents in equal measure among the enlightened communities of Amsterdam, Hamburg, and London and among the mystically inclined Jewries of Egypt, Syria, and Turkey. Such was the intensity of the movement that it deeply stirred even the non-Jewish world. Bets were taken at Lloyds as to the date when Sabbatai Zevi would enter Jerusalem in glory. The Messianic conception had also played an important part in the readmission of the Jews to England, it being held by the Puritan theologians that such resettlement was a necessary preliminary to the Jewish restoration in Palestine.

Much of this enthusiasm, Jewish and Christian, was millenarian mysticism, but the practical and rationalist spirit of the age also tended to direct it into more constructive channels. Already one of the late pseudo-Messiahs, David Reubeni, who in the early sixteenth century disturbed the communities of the West with an alleged appeal from the Jewish princes in Arabia for a joint reconquest of Palestine by European and Arabian Jews, had apparently been the protagonist of a secular Messianism. His aim was not so much the setting up of the Kingdom of God as the re-establishment of a Jewish state in Palestine.

A considerable number of political visionaries, Jewish and Christian, from the seventeenth to the nineteenth centuries pleaded for the restoration of the Jews and the re-establishment of a Jewish state in Palestine. Among such protagonists were the Danish merchant Paulli, who submitted elaborate schemes to King William III of England, Louis XIV of France, and other European monarchs; the French priest Pierre Jurieux; and the Prince de Ligne who, in 1797, published a lengthy memorandum in which he pleaded for the re-establishment of the Kingdom of Judaea in Palestine, arguing that such a restoration would benefit both Palestine and the Jews and would also improve the position of those of the race who remained in the Diaspora. It is well known that when Napoleon invaded Egypt and Syria in 1799, he published an appeal to the Jews of Asia and Africa inviting them "to join his colours in order to restore ancient Jerusalem." A "letter addressed to his brethren by a Jew," which was published in the preceding year by a French Jew and which indicates that the ideal of a Jewish return to Palestine was at the time popular also among French Jews, may have inspired Napoleon to issue his proclamation.

The hope and expectation of the restoration of Jerusalem and the Holy Land to the Jewish people were alive in the hearts of many Christians. The following Mormon prayer may serve as an example:

Now, O Lord! Thy servant has been obedient to the heavenly vision which thou gavest him in his native land; and under the shadow of thine out-stretched arm, he has safely arrived in this place to dedicate and consecrate this land unto thee, for the gathering together of Judah's scattered remnants, according to the prediction of the holy prophets—for the building up of Jerusalem again after it has been trodden down by the Gentiles so long, and for rearing a temple in honor of thy name. . . .

Grant therefore, O Lord, to remove the barrenness and sterility of this land, and let springs of living water break forth to water the thirsty soil. Let the vine and olive produce in their strength, and the fig-tree bloom and flourish. Let the land become abundantly fruitful when possessed by its rightful heirs. . . . Incline them to gather in upon this land according to thy word. Let them come like clouds and like doves to their windows. Let the large ships of the nations bring them from the distant isles; and let kings become their nursing fathers, and queens with motherly fondness wipe the tear of sorrow from their eye.

Thou, O Lord, did once move upon the heart of Cyrus to show favor unto Jerusalem and her children. Do thou also be pleased to inspire the hearts of kings and the powers of the earth to look with a friendly eye toward this place, and with a desire to see thy righteous purposes executed in relation thereto. Let them know that it is thy good pleasure to restore the kingdom unto Israel—raise up Jerusalem as its capital, and constitute her people a distinct nation and government, with David thy servant even a descendant from the loins of ancient David to be their king.

Let that nation or that people who shall take an active part in the behalf of Abraham's children; and in the raising up of Jerusalem, find favor in thy sight. Let not their enemies prevail against them, neither let pestilence or famine overcome them but let the glory of Israel overshadow them, and the power of the highest protect them; while that nation or kingdom that will not serve thee in this glorious work must perish, according to thy word: "Yea, those nations shall be utterly wasted."[8]

In the course of the centuries there have been many suggestions to solve the economic, national, cultural problems of the Jews who have suffered from discrimination and persecution in many lands by settling them in compact masses in some territories with autonomous or semiautonomous forms of government.

In the nineteenth century the vision of the return of the Jews to the land was revived with great force by numerous Jews and Christians all over the world. Mordecai Emanuel Noah—who first made an attempt, which failed, to estab-

[8] *A Sketch of the Travels and Ministry of Elder Orson Hyde* (Salt Lake City, 1869), pp. 20–22. See also Marvin Sidney Hill, *An Historical Study of the Life of Orson Hyde, Early Mormon Missionary and Apostle, from 1805–1852* (Typescript, 1955), pp. 43–65, 113–118.

lish on Grand Island, near Buffalo, a city of refuge for Jews, to be called Ararat—advocated the foundation of a state in Palestine. Sir Moses Montefiore, traveling in Palestine in May, 1839, conceived the idea of colonization near Tiberias. In England Sir Lawrence Oliphant, British Consul in Jerusalem, and Warder Cresson advocated a national home for the Jews.

When Mehemet Ali, the Viceroy of Egypt, overran Syria in 1832, the question of the political future of Palestine became an international issue. It was suggested that a Jewish buffer state be set up in Palestine between Turkey and Egypt.

The most notable advocate of a Jewish restoration was the seventh Earl of Shaftesbury (1801–1885). In 1838, he pleaded for the five powers of the West to enable the Jews to return and settle in Palestine, seeing that "everything seems ripe for their return." In an article published in the following year in the *Quarterly Review,* he developed the subject in greater detail, stating that he had learned on good authority that thousands of Jews in Poland and Russia had "recently bound themselves by oath that as soon as the way is open for them they will immediately go thither," and recording that the same sentiments had been expressed by Jewries in India and "in the remotest quarters of Asia."

During the London Convention of 1840, Lord Shaftesbury addressed a memorandum on the subject to Lord Palmerston. In an article published in the *Times* of August

79

17, 1840, it was stated that "the proposition to plant the Jewish people in the land of their fathers, under the protection of the five Powers, is no longer a mere matter of speculation, but of serious political consideration." On August 26, the *Times* printed the earlier memorandum in full, together with encouraging replies from most of the sovereigns addressed. A further memorandum on the subject appeared later in the year, voicing the opinion of a group of statesmen, in which the view was expounded that "the cause of the Restoration of the Jews to Palestine is one essentially generous and noble," that the colonization of Palestine by the Jews would be a remedy for contemporary conflicts, and that "it would be a crowning point in the glory of England to bring about such an event."

The subject continued to engage public opinion. "Palmerston was not unfriendly, but there was no Jewish organisation capable of handling so big a matter, and so the ambitious project was whittled down to the official protection by England of Jews in the East. And yet, this concession has proved by no means insignificant, for it is the logical precursor of Mr. Balfour's Declaration of November 1917."[9]

The idea of the return of the Jewish people to Palestine was cherished by many prominent figures in literature. Lord Byron, e.g., in his "Hebrew Melodies" gave moving

9 N. Sokolow, *History of Zionism*, Vol. I, pp. 15, 129.

expression to both the homelessness of the people and their attachment to the land:

The white dove hath her nest, the fox his cave,
Mankind their country, Israel but the grave.

Disraeli in his novel *Tancred;* George Eliot in *Daniel Deronda;* Alexandre Dumas the younger in *La Femme Claude,* in the words of one of his characters, pleaded for the return of the land to the Jews. It was above all Moses Hess in *Rome and Jerusalem* and Leo Pinsker in *Auto-Emancipation* and later Theodor Herzl who pleaded for the establishment of a Jewish state.

In 1903, Joseph Chamberlain on behalf of the British Government suggested that Theodor Herzl settle the Jews in Uganda (now Kenya). In 1928, the Soviet Union announced its plan to settle the Russian Jews in Birobijan. All these projects proved flimsy and incapable of fulfillment. The Jewish masses did not respond to these projects. The dream, the hope, the certainty of returning to the land of Israel was so deeply ingrained in the Jewish soul that any other project had a tinge of illegitimacy. Over and above that, the lands considered were either unavailable or totally unsuited.

"Philologists have argued whether Sir Thomas More, who called his ideal State Utopia, meant Eutopia, a good

81

place, or Outopia, no place. There is no doubt that when kind friends offer us substitutes for Palestine they mean Outopia, nowhere. They may give it a geographical name, fluttering on the winds of chance from Madagascar to Libya or Guiana, but as soon as you attempt to pin it down it reveals itself as nowhere and the pin is lost in the void."[10]

On November 2, 1917, the British Government issued the Balfour Declaration, which stated that "His Majesty's Government view with favour the establishment in Palestine of a national home for the Jewish people . . . ," thus recognizing the historic right of the Jews to a national home in Palestine.

The Balfour Declaration was adopted by the San Remo Conference, April, 1920, as a "declaration of sympathy for Jewish Zionist aspirations" and there the Principal Allied Powers granted Great Britain a Mandate over Palestine, which was confirmed and defined by the League of Nations in 1922. Great Britain, to which the administration of Palestine was turned over, was charged by Article 4 of the Mandate "to secure the cooperation of all Jews who are willing to assist in the establishment of a Jewish National Home" in Palestine.

The Mandate in its Preamble recognizes the historic

[10] Harry Sachar, "Palestine or Outopia," *Manchester Guardian,* May, 1943.

connection of the Jewish people with Palestine and "the grounds for *reconstituting* their national home in that country."

These international commitments in which the thought and conscience of mankind came to expression flowed from the recognition of historic rights of the Jewish people and present needs.

The meaning of the Mandate was to culminate in the establishment of a Jewish Commonwealth. Thus President Woodrow Wilson on March 3, 1919, stated "that the Allied Nations with the fullest concern of our own government and people are agreed that in Palestine shall be laid the foundation of a Jewish Commonwealth."

It was upon these international commitments that the Jewish people dedicated human, economic, and spiritual resources to the upbuilding of the land. What the Jewish people, inspired by the hope of reconstituting their national home after the long, weary homelessness and relying on the honor and pledged word of the world community, has achieved in a few short years against great odds and seemingly insurmountable physical handicaps has won the acclaim of the entire world.

What was built with social vision and the spirit of idealism has proved a blessing not only to the Jews but to the Arabs of the land whose standard of living, including health and education, far surpasses the standards of the Arabs in the entire Middle East.

In 1947, a special United Nations committee proposed that the Mandate be terminated and Palestine divided into two sovereign states, one Jewish and the other Arab, and that Jerusalem be internationalized. The Partition Plan was adopted by the General Assembly on November 29, 1947, by a vote of 33 to 13. The Jews accepted it, the Arabs rejected it, and on May 14, 1948, the State of Israel was proclaimed.

It was the leadership of David Ben-Gurion that was largely responsible for the implementation of the United Nations resolution of November, 1947, recommending the establishment of a Jewish state in part of Palestine. In April, 1948, he was placed at the head of the provisional government which, in May, 1948, proclaimed the creation of the State of Israel.

EMISSARIES

Those who dwelt in other lands have at all times sought to strengthen the Jewish settlements in the land. Their support was considered a sacred responsibility. In every age the leaders of the Jewish people everywhere were engaged in activities for their benefit. An important role in carrying out such activities was played by so-called "messengers" from the Holy Land who would regularly visit Jewish communities all over the world to receive contributions.

The institutions of "messengers" seems to have continued without interruption for nearly nineteen hundred years since the destruction of the Temple. Their message was subject to change due to changing conditions. Their character, pathos, and purpose remained unaltered throughout the centuries: to cultivate spiritual attachment to the Holy Land. There was no need for these messengers to plead for contributions—every Jew regarded it as his most meaningful duty and privilege to have a share in Jewish living in the Holy Land. The messenger was not only a

85

recipient; he brought gifts of inspiration, moral guidance, and consolation. Among these messengers were some of the greatest scholars and mystics in the land of Israel. They were listened to as having special authority. They often changed customs and liturgies and made decisions in local affairs. A person coming from the Holy Land was himself endowed with the charisma of the land.

These messengers realized that their role was beyond the purpose of collecting contributions. The messenger is the representative of the living land and has to exemplify the best qualities of those who live in the presence of God in the land. He has to bring the illumination and the comfort of the land of Israel to those who dwell in the dark misery of exile; to arouse intense craving for redemption in the hearts of those whose faith may slumber.

The messenger would tell not only of the economic difficulties of the Jews living in the land, but above all of the land itself, its holiness, its marvels, its sages, its saints, its customs, its habits, the grace and reminders of ancient splendor. Every messenger was a treasure house of legends about the qualities, miracles, and signs of redemption which appeared on the Temple Mount, about the ten lost tribes who really lived in the wild places across the Holy Land, about the high merit of those who dwell in the land and of those who support them. They would teach songs and melodies from the Holy Land, thus deepening the nostalgia. They would bring samples of the soil and distin-

guished individuals would each receive a packet of this
earth. Messengers played a major role in bringing the
writings and ideas of the great mystics Rabbi Moshe Cordovero (d. 1570) and Rabbi I. Luria (d. 1572) of Safed to
the Jews of other lands.

It was held that every Jew was under religious obligation
to live in Palestine, but since this was impossible to the
majority, a system of regular contribution toward the support of an elite of learned settlers in Palestine—the so-called
Halukah—was established throughout the congregations
of the Diaspora, the individual being, as it were, "repre-
sented" in the Holy Land by those whom he maintained
by his support. The underlying conception of "representation" was emphasized by the organization of the
system on territorial lines, each country being responsible
for a distinct group of settlers, whereby a note of local
attachment was introduced.

In almost every home there was a box for donations
toward the maintenance of Jewish communities in the
Holy Land. Before kindling the lights in greeting the arrival of the Sabbath, the woman of the house would drop a
coin into the box specified for the purpose of maintaining
the poor in the Holy Land.[11] The boxes were usually
called "Money for Erets Israel" and, in some Karaite com-

[11] On the role in history of the emissaries, see Abraham Yaari, *Sheluhei
Erets Israel* (Jerusalem, 1951).

munities, "If I Forget Thee . . . ." In the list of contributions from the city of Nuremburg, for the years 1373 to 1392, donations for the poor people of Jews were mentioned. Especially was it common to offer such contributions on the three festivals. These contributions were sent to duly elected treasurers, who were usually in charge of receiving money from an entire country. To be elected treasurer was considered a high honor.[12]

In the time of emergency, of economic deterioration in the land, when it was felt that the voluntary contributions were not sufficient, a kind of taxation was instituted, such as in the year 1601 in Venice and apparently in other cities of Italy, and in 1727 in Constantinople. In every community, the treasurer elected for the purpose received donations, arranged campaigns at festive occasions and on special days in the year, and arranged for giving money to a messenger or sending it to a national treasurer, or directly to Erets Israel. In some communities there were special societies, the members of which regularly contributed to Israel. Such societies existed in Rome, e.g., in 1670.

[12] Isaac Rifkind, *Jewish Money in Folkways, Cultural History and Folklore: A Lexicological Study* (New York: American Academy for Jewish Research, 1959), p. 38.

3

Between hope
and distress

HOPE

Why did our hearts throughout the ages turn to Erets Israel, to the Holy Land? Because of hope, because of memory, because of distress.

Because of hope. Over and above the deep sadness of our melodies, fears and experience of persecutions, rituals of mourning and memories of sorrow, hovers the power of hope.

Hope is our power. It is a vital quality always at work within a person, anticipating freedom from misery. It is a power of perception, an intuition, a foreseeing.

Hope cannot stand alone. It must be morally substantiated, faithfully attended. It must not lose the element of constancy and the intensity of expectancy.

93

Hope is *not* cheerfulness, a temperamental confidence that all will turn out for the best. It is *not* an inclination to be guided by illusions rather than by facts. Hope is a conviction, rooted in trust, trust in Him who issued the promise; an ability to soar above the darkness that overshadows the divine.

Our people were not carried away by despair because Jewish faith is not simply faith in a supreme being called God. Our faith is trust in Him who is in need of man, involved with all of us, remembering and waiting for His promise to come to pass.

Out of the Bible comes a voice: You shall be patient, for I the Lord your God am patient.

Jewish hope continued as yearning and expectation, as waiting and anticipation. Perhaps the most characteristic quality of Jewish existence is *bittahon* ("hope"). Believing and hoping are one. It is part of our very existence to be faithful to the future, to keep alive the beginning by nursing the vision of the end. Hope is the creative articulation of faith. We misunderstand events past unless we are certain of events to come.

Nothing seemed as elusive, as unsustainable as the prospect of the restoration of Zion at the time of the Crusades, e.g., during the *autos-da-fé* of the Spanish Inquisition, or during the pogroms of Chmielnicki in 1648–49. Entertaining such a hope could only evoke scorn and derision among those who despised us. For two thousand years the Jewish people persisted in hoping, in waiting, in praying. In the eyes of the cynics, it was a senseless dream; in the eyes of God, an all-absorbing prayer.

Zionism was born out of memory, out of ritual and prayer, out of faith in the promise, out of loyalty to the biblical command, never to forget our origin, our link, never to relinquish hope for Zion and Jerusalem.

To the Jews in the Soviet Union who wonder when their cultural and religious oppression will end, when the world will become psychologically secure, it is a source of strength when they turn their thoughts to Israel.

The first step in the modern and planned return to the land was to establish an agricultural school near Jaffa in 1869. Its name was Mikveh Israel, "the hope of Israel" (Jeremiah 14:8), while the name of the first agricultural colony was Petah Tikvah, "the door of hope" (Hosea 2:17). The national anthem of the Zionist movement and the State of Israel is *Hatikvah* ("The Hope").

The strength of faith is in silence, and in words that hibernate and wait. Uttered faith must come out as surplus of silence, as creative deeds are the fruit of enduring patience.

WAITING

Trust is not an irrespective attitude of reliance on another person's integrity. Trust is the intimate reflection and outcome of another person's integrity, continuously dependent upon it. The person in whom I trust is present in my trust.

Our waiting for the restoration of Jerusalem is a reflection of God's integrity, continuously depending upon it. Our trust *is* His presence. "Blessed is the man who trusts in the Lord, whose trust *is* the Lord" (Jeremiah 17:7). Trust in God *is* God.[1]

To wait is to stay in readiness, to live a life of expectation. To be able to wait one must prepare for the arriving. Waiting for Him becomes waiting with Him, sharing in the coming.

Waiting is vital to biblical faith. The Lord "works for those who wait for Him" (Isaiah 64:3; rsv, vs. 4).

Man is not alone in his waiting. ". . . the Lord waits to

[1] Deuteronomy Rabba, 1, 12.

be gracious to you. . . . blessed are all those who wait for him" (Isaiah 30:18). "I will wait for the Lord, who is hiding his face from the house of Jacob, and I will hope in him" (Isaiah 8:17).

For still the vision awaits its time;
It hastens to the end—it will not lie.
If it seem slow, wait for it;
It will surely come, it will not delay.

Habakkuk 2:3

"Blessed is he who waits . . ." (Daniel 12:12).

Waiting did not mean a state of repose or inaction, putting off activity until later; it meant, rather, that the success of all human efforts toward redemption remained contingent and indecisive without God's action. While the world was chiding, Israel persisted in its dream. Religious Zionism maintained that Israel's initiative must open the power of redemption, that waiting must not be separated from pioneering.

What is required of a Jew is more than assurance, more than inert waiting; what is required is looking-for, expectancy, awaiting redemption. When man is led in for judgment (in the next world), we are told that he is asked: Did you hope intensely for salvation?[2]

---

[2] Shabbat, 31a.

"Prepare yourselves for salvation!"[3] Jewish faith is a faith of expectation.

> *Out of the depths, I cry to thee, O Lord.*
>   *Lord hear my voice! . . .*
> *I wait for the Lord, my soul waits,*
>   *and in his word I hope;*
> *my soul waits for the Lord*
>   *more than watchmen for the morning,*
>   *more than watchmen for the morning.*
>
>   *Psalm 130:1–2, 5–6*

"This is what the prophets discovered. *History is a nightmare.* There are more scandals, more acts of corruption, than are dreamed of in philosophy. It would be blasphemous to believe that what we witness is the end of God's creation. It is an act of evil to accept the state of evil as either inevitable or final. Others may be satisfied with improvement, the prophets insist upon redemption. The way man acts is a disgrace, and it must not go on forever. Together with condemnation, the prophets offer a promise. The heart of stone will be taken away, a heart of flesh will be given instead (Ezek. 11:19). Even the nature of the beasts will change to match the glory of the age. The end of days will be the end of fear, the end of war; idolatry will disappear, knowledge of God will prevail.

---

[3] Genesis Rabba, 98, 2, ed. Theodor, p. 1250.

"The inner history of Israel is a history of waiting for God, of waiting for His arrival. Just as Israel is certain of the reality of the Promised Land, so is she certain of the coming of 'the promised day.' She lives by a promise of 'the day of the Lord,' a day of judgment followed by salvation, when evil will be consumed and an age of glory will ensue."[4]

Believing Jews would daily confess: "I firmly believe in the coming of the Messiah; and although he may tarry, I daily wait for his coming."

PROMISE

The Bible is the book of anticipations. The ground for the hope is in the promise. The future has a face, and in its face you see the glory.

[4] Abraham J. Heschel, *The Prophets* (New York: Harper & Row, 1962), p. 181.

There is evil, there is anguish. There is death, agony, exile. But beyond all darkness is the dawn.

"On this mountain the Lord of hosts will make for all peoples a feast . . . . And he will destroy on this mountain the covering that is cast over all peoples, the veil that is spread over all nations. He will swallow up death for ever, and the Lord God will wipe away tears from all faces, and the reproach of his people he will take away from all the earth; for the Lord has spoken. It will be said on that day, 'Lo, this is our God; we have waited for him, that he might save us. This is the Lord; we have waited for him; let us be glad and rejoice in his salvation' " (Isaiah 25:6–9).

The evil state of the world, with its ugliness and violence, will not endure forever. At the end of days, in a climax of days, there will be a new dawn of history. Redemption will come, cleansing the world from war and hatred. This is God's pledge and Israel's hope. At the same time, biblical eschatology and all our hopes for the future are mysteriously centered in the Holy Land.

There is a unique association between the people and the land of Israel. Even before Israel becomes a people, the land is preordained for Israel.

Even before there was a people, there was a promise. The promise of a land. The election of Abraham and the election of the land came together. The promise of the land to the patriarchs is the leit motif in the Five Books of

100

Moses. Israel's claim upon Canaan goes back to the earliest period of its history and was thought of as having its origin in the will of God, since it was to the Lord that this land belonged and He alone could dispose of it.

Beyond the promise of the land and increasing posterity, the promise to Abraham was a blessing for all the families of the earth. The gift of the land is an earnest of a greater promise.

The granting of the land of Canaan to Israel by the Lord is a theme reflected upon again and again. "Then he brought us to this place and gave us this land, a land flowing with milk and honey" (Deuteronomy 26:9). Thanksgiving for this grant remained alive in never-ending praise throughout biblical history.

Pagans have idols, Israel has a promise. We have no image, all we have is hope.

Israel reborn is a verification of the promise.

History goes on in time as well as in space, and according to biblical faith, the promise of redemption of all peoples involves the presence of this people in this land.

The books of the Bible reverberate with the promise of return. "The Lord your God will restore your fortunes, and have compassion upon you, and he will gather you again from all the peoples where the Lord your God has scattered you. If your outcasts are in the uttermost parts of heaven, from there the Lord your God will gather you, and from

101

there he will fetch you; and the Lord your God will bring you into the land which your fathers possessed" (Deuteronomy 30:3–5).

> *"I will restore the fortunes of my people Israel,*
> *and they shall rebuild the ruined cities and inhabit them;*
> *they shall plant vineyards and drink their wine,*
> *and they shall make gardens and eat their fruit.*
> *I will plant them upon their land,*
> *and they shall never again be plucked up*
> *out of the land which I have given them,"*
> *says the Lord your God.*

Amos 9:14–15

Every Jew, whoever and wherever he was, heard in the words of Scripture the mighty voice of the Lord of nature and history.

"Thus says the Lord: I will return to Zion, and will dwell in the midst of Jerusalem, and Jerusalem shall be called the faithful city, and the mountain of the Lord of hosts, the holy mountain. Thus says the Lord of hosts: Old men and old women shall again sit in the streets of Jerusalem, each with staff in hand for every age.

"And the streets of the city shall be full of boys and girls playing in its streets. . . . and I will bring [my people] to

102

dwell in the midst of Jerusalem; and they shall be my people and I will be their God, in faithfulness and righteousness" (Zechariah 8:3–8).

The Hebrew Bible does not use the word "promise" in relation to the land but, rather, a term much stronger, namely "to swear." To promise is to give assurance without suggesting further grounds for expectation for the fulfillment of what is promised. To swear means to declare solemnly under oath, or on one's word of honor. See Genesis 26:3; Exodus 33:1; Numbers 14:23; 23:11; Deuteronomy 1:35, and many more passages. The term "the promise of God" appears in Judaism prior to Paul. The term "the land of the promise" is found in Hebrews 11:9.[5]

[5] On *Epaggelia* in the New Testament see *Theological Dictionary of the New Testament,* edited by Gerhard Kittel (Grand Rapids, Mich.: Wm. B. Eerdmans, 1956), Vol. II, pp. 576 ff.

DISTRESS

As I have said, Jews went to the land of Israel out of hope, out of memory, out of distress.

The last century in Jewish history was an age of distress, an age of unparalleled suffering. A new situation arose, calling for moving from dream to deed.

And events are louder than words, and bitter events shocked us into the realization that return to Zion was a necessity. What was desired proved to be required. What was cherished as a hope emerged as a demand.

Zionism at the beginning impressed many people as a poetic idea, as a romantic vision. Shunning pragmatism, it proclaimed an impossible program: the transfer of a people from civilized Europe to a country full of swamps and rocks, to a trying climate, with no opportunities of employment.

To translate a hope into a program of action the Zionist movement had to awaken a people that had become resigned to national helplessness, to the possibility and necessity of self-emancipation. In order to rebuild the land it had

104

to rebuild the mind of the people. To have brought about such a transformation is one of the major achievements of the movement.

It called for public purchase of land as the inalienable property of the Jewish people—land to be leased to settlers, never sold, never placed on the market. In short, nationalization by purchase. It was a genuinely idealistic measure, and it was inspired far more by the ancient Jewish relationship to the meaning of land than by modern single-tax or socialist theories.

The crisis was grave. Was the Jewish people properly equipped to face cataclysmic changes? To confront reality? Zionism was a call to courage, a test of character, a risk, putting all our qualities to the test.

It challenged an old people to help itself, to mobilize and to employ dormant faculties of which the people was not aware.

Jewish life had been menaced by mockery and oppression, by pogroms, poverty, assimilation. The situation called for initiative, for radical action. God himself will not save men against their will. What is implicit today in the calls for anti-poverty programs, for urban renewal, was even more urgent in the call for return to Zion. So many of our people were called to leave their homeland, like Abraham of old. They went to Palestine, purchased land that had lain desolate for nearly two thousand years, cultivated the soil and converted deserts into gardens.

The last decades of the nineteenth century witnessed the

105

rise of anti-Semitism as an organized movement in Germany. The spring of 1881 initiated the age of pogroms in Russia. Trials of ritual murder were organized in 1882 in Tisza-Eszlar, Hungary; in 1914 against Beilis in Kiev, Russia. The Dreyfus affair in France at the end of the century came as a thunderbolt. Meanwhile the promulgations of restricting laws against the Jews in Russia drove the masses into misery.

I have said that the last century of Jewish history was an age of distress. However, beginning with 1933, when the Nazis came to power, the Jews on the continent of Europe moved from an age of distress to an age of disaster.

1938 . . . 1939 . . . What was the situation of millions of Jews in the lands of the continent of Europe? We have lived in some parts of Europe for nearly two thousand years, labored, worshiped, studied, suffered, built, shed our blood in fighting for liberty and independence, contributed to science and literature, created forms of spiritual living. And now we found ourselves besieged by a fury of hatred and contempt, by a demonic rage, unprecedented in the annals of history.

The tempest of hatred raged in many lands. In Germany they screamed, "Death to the Jews! Death to the Jews!" And there was nowhere to go.

Homeless we sat in the corridors of all foreign consulates. We knocked at the doors, we sent out appeals. But the answer was *"No!"* There was no refuge, no way of escape from the inferno.

106

Ships with illegal cargoes of escaping Jews wandered about the world, unable to make port because no port was open to them. They were hunted down in the Mediterranean and if one of them beached on the Palestinian shore the passengers were arrested and deported.

Illegal boats. Illegal Jews. All ports sealed. All hearts closed. The drama of the Jewish people has lasted too long. Let us finish it once and for all. They are all here. Pharaoh screams, Titus triumphs, Chrysostom and Torquemada rejoice. Chmielnicki, Petlura are ready. Satan may relax. Nazis will kill and sing.

> *Even the sparrow finds a home,*
> *and the swallow a nest for herself,*
> *where she may lay her young, . . .*

Psalm 84:3

but we Jews had nowhere to lay our heads. The forests all over the world, the mansions, the valleys so boastfully beautiful, where so many mothers could have found a hiding place to save children from being sent to the gas chambers, remained deaf to the cry of anguish.

We were trapped. The gates of all continents were closed, and the gates of extermination camps opened.

Surely one of the most characteristic phenomena of our time is the denial of asylum to those persecuted for religious or political reasons. History has known nothing

107

like it. The Jews driven from Spain found shelter in the Sultan's empire and in the Netherlands Republic; the Huguenots fleeing France settled in the colonies of the New World, or in the Prussian Kingdom; but "displaced persons" are an essentially modern phenomenon. Countries did not grant visas to poverty-stricken German Jews, or gave them only with extreme reluctance. In response to public opinion and following various interventions, President Franklin D. Roosevelt of the United States called an international conference on July 6, 1938, at Evian, to do something about this problem. But the only result of the Evian conference was the creation of a permanent inter-governmental committee with headquarters in London; its representatives regularly went to Berlin to arrange for the financing of emigration through property requisitioned from the Jews. But these attempts failed because the powers of the intergovernmental committee were very limited, and the nations making it up, divided in their counsels and their minds, did not really know what they wanted.[6]

[6] Leon Poliakov, *Harvest of Hate* (London: Elek Books, 1956), p. 26; see also Arthur D. Morse, *While Six Million Died,* A Chronicle of American Apathy (New York: Random House, 1967).

THE MIRACLE OF THE RESURRECTION

"The hand of the Lord was upon me, and he brought me out by the Spirit of the Lord, and set me down in the midst of the valley; it was full of bones. And he led me round among them; and behold, there were very many upon the valley; and lo, they were very dry. And he said to me, 'Son of man, can these bones live?' And I answered, 'O Lord God, thou knowest.' Again he said to me, 'Prophesy to these bones, and say to them, O dry bones, hear the word of the Lord. Thus says the Lord God to these bones: Behold, I will cause breath to enter you, and you shall live. And I will lay sinews upon you, and will cause flesh to come upon you, and cover you with skin, and put breath in you, and you shall live; and you shall know that I am the Lord.'

"So I prophesied as I was commanded; and as I prophesied, there was a noise, and behold, a rattling; and the bones came together, bone to its bone. And as I looked, there were sinews on them, and flesh had come upon them,

109

and skin had covered them; but there was no breath in them. Then he said to me, 'Prophesy to the breath, prophesy, son of man, and say to the breath, Thus says the Lord God: Come from the four winds, O breath, and breathe upon these slain, that they may live.' So I prophesied as he commanded me, and the breath came into them, and they lived, and stood upon their feet, an exceedingly great host.

"Then he said to me, 'Son of man, these bones are the whole house of Israel. Behold, they say, Our bones are dried up, and our hope is lost; we are clean cut off. Therefore prophesy, and say to them, Thus says the Lord God: Behold I will open your graves, and raise you from your graves, O my people; and I will bring you home into the land of Israel. And you shall know that I am the Lord, when I open your graves, and raise you from your graves, O my people. And I will put my Spirit within you, and you shall live, and I will place you in your own land; then you shall know that I, the Lord, have spoken, and I have done it, says the Lord.' " (Ezekiel 37:1–14.)

DISASTER

1945 . . . A new conception: The world is a slaughter-house. Hope is obscene. It is sinful to remain sane.

Six million lives gone. Wherever we dwell, we live in a graveyard. Only one way out, the way to the inferno.

1945 . . . Is this what is left of us: chimneys in the extermination camps?

What shall come after the holocaust: nights of despair, no dawn, never, but shrieks in perpetuity? Anguish forever, no relief, life is gall, history a scourge? Has the world lost its soul? Have civilization and humanity nothing in common?

Has Auschwitz annihilated our future as well?

Three out of four Jews in Europe—dead. Two out of five of us anywhere in the world—dead. Will the spirit of those who survived be reduced to ashes? The Allied Armies which freed the concentration camps came upon tens of thousands of emaciated bodies, skeletons, dry bones. "Son of man, can these bones live?" Judaism was reduced to dry

111

bones, faith in God was on trial. Will this people, crushed, battered, crippled, decimated, impaled, find strength to survive?

What should have been our answer to Auschwitz? Should this people, called to be a witness to the God of mercy and compassion, persist in its witness and cling to Job's words: "Even if He slay me yet will I trust in Him" (Job 13:15), or should this people follow the advice of Job's wife, "Curse God and die!" (Job 2:9), immerse itself into the anonymity of a hundred nations all over the world, and disappear once and for all?

Our people's faith in God at this moment in history did not falter. At this moment in history Isaac was indeed sacrificed, his blood shed. We all died in Auschwitz, yet our faith survived. We knew that to repudiate God would be to continue the holocaust.

We have once lived in a civilized world, rich in trust and expectation. Then we all died, were condemned to dwell in hell. Now we are living in hell. Our present life is our after-life. . . .

We did not blaspheme, we built. Our people did not sally forth in flight from God. On the contrary, at that moment in history we saw the beginning of a new awakening, the emergence of a new concern for a Living God theology. Escape from Judaism giving place increasingly to a new attachment, to a rediscovery of our legacy.

How would the world have looked at the Jewish people if

112

the survivors of the concentration camps had gone the path of complete assimilation? Flight from God? From Judaism?

What would be the face of Western history today if the end of twentieth-century Jewish life would have been Bergen-Belsen, Dachau, Auschwitz? The State of Israel is not an atonement. It would be blasphemy to regard it as a compensation. However, the existence of Israel reborn makes life less unendurable. It is a slight hinderer of hindrances to believing in God.

We are tired of expulsions, of pogroms; we have had enough of extermination camps. We are tired of apologizing for our existence. If I should go to Poland or Germany, every stone, every tree would remind me of contempt, hatred, murder, of children killed, of mothers burned alive, of human beings asphyxiated.

When I go to Israel every stone and every tree is a reminder of hard labor and glory, of prophets and psalmists, of loyalty and holiness. The Jews go to Israel not only for physical security for themselves and their children; they go to Israel for renewal, for the experience of resurrection.

Is the State of Israel God's humble answer to Auschwitz? A sign of God's repentance for men's crime of Auschwitz?

No act is as holy as the act of saving human life. The Holy Land, having offered a haven to more than two million Jews—many of whom would not have been alive had they remained in Poland, Russia, Germany, and other countries—has attained a new sanctity.

So many lives of people whose bodies were injured and whose souls were crushed found a new life and a new spirit in the land. The State of Israel, as it were, sought to respond to the prophet's exhortation: "Strengthen the weak hands, and make firm the feeble knees" (Isaiah 35:3).

In 1937, the period of Nazi persecution and expulsion of the Jews from Germany, I concluded a book about Don Isaac Abravanel, who lived during the time of the expulsion of the Jews from Spain in 1492, with the following words:

The Jews, who had played a leading role in the politics, economics and social affairs of their country left (had to leave) their Spanish homeland. The conquest of the New World was achieved without them. Had they remained on the Iberian peninsula they would surely have participated in the deeds of the Conquistadores. When the latter came to Haiti they found 1,100,000 inhabitants; twenty years later only 1,000 remained.[7]

In 1492 the Jews, who were desperate, had no inkling what an act of grace was involved in their misery. Driven out of Spain, they had no part in the atrocities soon to be carried out in the New World.

[7] Abraham J. Heschel, *Don Jizchak Abravanel* (Berlin: Erich Reiss, 1937), p. 30.

114

And yet, there is no answer to Auschwitz. . . . To try to answer is to commit a supreme blasphemy. Israel enables us to bear the agony of Auschwitz without radical despair, to sense a ray of God's radiance in the jungles of history.

PIONEERS

Mourning, love, and longing do not build a land.

The hour called for toil, skill, and will. So a miracle had happened. Tens, then hundreds, and then thousands of youth left large and small towns of eastern Europe and went into the wilderness of the ancient land, ready to toil and to build, to labor and to sing.

History was knocking at our doors. The pioneers heard it and answered. The path was steep. Yet they achieved prodigies.

To the eyes of the practical-minded people the efforts of the pioneers were foolish, futile. The stumbling-blocks, the

115

snags, seemed insurmountable. There was no security to life and property.

Hard, strenuous labor; modest gains, no security to life and labor. As at the time of Nehemiah, the opponents said, "What are these feeble Jews doing? Will they restore things? . . . Will they revive the stones out of the heaps of rubbish, and burned ones at that?" (Nehemiah 3:34; RSV, 4:2).

What motivated the pioneers in going to the grim, withered land? There were both negative and positive reasons. There was the protest against exile, the protest against pogroms and living in fear of pogroms, of expulsions, discrimination, defenselessness. As individuals they could attain freedom, success, independence, dignity, yet they insisted upon finding freedom, independence, dignity, for their people.

Another motivation—among those who had lived in Czarist Russia—was the rejection of the exploitative economy, as well as their vision of a just social order.

They were the salt of the earth, zealous, yet modest; patient of hardship; serene amid alarms; inflexible in faith; no dangers frightened them, no labors tired them. They had a vision: building a home for a homeless people.

Noncompetitive, nonambitious, their aspiration was to live a life of justice and simplicity. Spurning all afterthoughts of profit or personal reward, of career and success,

116

believing in the holiness of physical labor, they established small collectives, drained swamps, cleared the land of rocks and stones, nursed plants, raised cattle, fowl. It was a path of austerity as well as of joy in revealing the beauty and vitality hidden beneath the surface of a deserted land.

The pioneers were moved by a vision of the future, as well as by a love of the soil. The things that evoked enthusiasm were a tree planted, a garden cultivated, a road cut across a field, a haystack at harvest time. They lived with the cows and the sheep, and sensed a divine halo hovering over simple things of soil. The draining of a swamp was an act of redemptive connotation. One cannot appreciate the land rebuilt unless one remembers the land in ruins, the cities laid waste, the land desolate.

At the time of Moses the Israelites had to spend forty years in the wilderness before entering the Promised Land. This time the land itself was wilderness, "a barren waste, a wild of sand."

Ancient cities erased, fields desolate, the soil forsaken, unloved by its inhabitants. Instead of "flowing with milk and honey," it was a land teeming with ruins, infested with malaria, a country without trees.

Any man who traveled from Dan to Beersheba would cry: this is all arid, hopelessly sterile.

Indeed, Zionism was a dream, a Utopia. Practical people could not but scoff at those who were ready to be intoxi-

117

cated with a mere dream, who left the fleshpots of Europe to settle in the sands of Palestine, to drain the swamps—in the process of which so many people died of malaria.

The Holy Land which some of the older people among us can still remember as a place of desolation and ruins has responded to the toil of the pioneers as if to carry out the prophet's prediction:

The wilderness and the dry land shall be glad,
the desert shall rejoice and blossom; . . .

Isaiah 35:1

The renewal of the land, the act of making the desert blossom, is bound to serve as an inspiration to underdeveloped lands all over the world.

Israel reborn is an answer to the Lord of history who demands hope as well as action, who expects tenacity as well as imagination.

THE LAND

What is so precious about the land? What is the magnetic quality of its atmosphere?

The land of Israel—biblical chapters hovering everywhere. Places like Hebrew letters, waiting to be vocalized, waiting for crowns with which to be adorned. The land is a text.

Here you are illiterate unless you remember words of Scripture. Wherever you stand you are at the frontier of biblical moments.

It is a land where the Bible is at home.

This tiny corner is the spot where the most sublime moments of encounter between God and man took place, where the most precious visions were born.

Many poets have claimed that the grandeur of heaven and earth is disclosed in this land in a special way. But even those whose ears are not fully opened to the silent song insist that just being in the land is a recalling. It is like being embraced by an air of spirit, challenging us into

119

the awareness that living in the land is a confrontation with the prophets who were able to hold God and man in one thought at one time, at all times.

We must seek to understand Israel reborn in the light of history, from the perspective of time. It is a land where not a spot is visible that is not reflecting an event, a moment.

The land is different. Those who built it and those who worship in it inspire it. It is an inspired land. Just to be in the land is a religious experience.

It is a land where time transcends space, where space is a dimension of time. When you think of Israel, you think of events, of breakthroughs in history.

Faith is a moment, the sight of a lightning. So difficult to retain. The land of Israel is memory, frozen faithfulness.

We cherish the air we breathe, but the air is not a fetish. Jewish history is a craving for the land, but the land is not a fetish, the potatoes that grow in its soil do not possess spiritual efficacy.

We do not worship the soil. The land of Israel without the God of Israel will be here today and gone tomorrow.

Zion, many lands are beautiful,
But no eye has seen the equal of thy beauty.
I know not whether the skies bow to thee,
Or whether thou ascendest to the skies.

Al-Harizi, thirteenth century

120

Israel is the one place in the world where there is no anti-Semitism—where there is no need for an Anti-Defamation League. It is a country where a full Jewish life can be lived in accord with tradition and conscience; where the Sabbath fills the streets, not only the homes; where the language is Hebrew. Israel is where the Jewish people face the complex challenge of the social and spiritual crises of the day, ready to give shelter to any Jews in distress.

Every people has a right to its own territory, in which it can develop its own culture and strive for making a contribution to the world out of its own spirit.

Israel's vital interest in peace has been expressed again and again.

What is holy about the Holy Land? It is not only because its space is filled with frozen echoes of a voice heard in the past. Erets Israel is a prelude, an anticipation. The Holy Land is regarded as the place where the divine plan of history can unfold its pristine and unique meaning.

The land of Israel has been sanctified by the words of the prophets, by the suffering of a whole people, by the tears and prayers of thousands of years, by the labor and dedication of pioneers. Such sanctity is precious to God, vital to the people, a light within history. The State of Israel is not only a place of refuge for the survivors of the holocaust, but also a tabernacle for the rebirth of faith and justice, for the renewal of souls, for the cultivation of

121

knowledge of the words of the divine. By the power and promise of prophetic visions we inhabit the land, by faithfulness to God and Torah we continue to survive.

The land presents a perception which seeks an identity in us. Suddenly we sense coherence in history, a bridge that spans the ages.

Israel reborn is an explicit rendering of an ineffable mystery. The Presence is cloudy, but the challenge is unmistakable.

This is part of our exultation: to witness the resurrection of the land of the Bible; a land that was dead for nearly two thousand years is now a land that sings.

4
Israel
and meaning
in history

MEMORY OF HISTORY

What lends meaning to history? The promise of the future. If there is no promise, there is no meaningful history. Significance is contingent on vision and anticipation, on living the future in the present tense.

This is one of the gifts of the Bible to the world: a promise, a vision, a hope.

History is not a flimsy course of disconnected happenings devoid of duration. History has a memory of moments. Man may forget, history remembers. Man has often tried to destroy history, yet again and again the memory of history bursts forth seeking to repair the absurdity caused by brutality and suicidal tendencies. It is the memory of history that holds together despair and hope, defiance and promise, in spite of the passion to refute all hope.

History, as we see it, is the alternation of frustration and hope; its memory is in cleaving to the promise. Man cannot live without a future. Man cannot live significantly without the past. Genuine history endures. "I know that whatever God does endures forever" (Ecclesiastes 3:14).

What *is* may vanish. Yet certain moments in history never vanish. There is a dimension of history in which a hidden force is moving silently, in which primordial material of commitment and experience is being molded into happenings.

We are a people in whom the past endures, in whom the present is inconceivable without moments gone by. The vision of the prophets lasted a moment, a moment enduring forever. What happened once upon a time happens all the time.

Abraham is still standing before the Lord, seeking to save Sodom and Gomorrah (Genesis 18:22). Nathan the prophet is still standing before David the king and saying: "You are the man!" (II Samuel 12:7.)

Time is not an empty dimension. It can be a palace of meaning if we know how to build it with precious deeds. Our imperishable homeland is in God's time. We enter God's time through the gate of sacred deeds. The deeds, acts of sanctifying time, are the old ancestral ground where we meet Him again and again. The great sacred deed for us today is to build the land of Israel.

128

"The universe is done. The greater masterpiece still undone, still in the process of being created: history. For accomplishing this grand design, God needs the help of man. Man is and has the instruments of God which he may or may not use in consonance with the grand design.

"Life is clay, and righteousness the mold in which God wants history to be shaped."[1]

Perhaps the meaning of the sin of the first man was in his having gone to nature to learn about good and evil. But the destiny of man is to learn from history the meaning of good and evil. For us to stand aloof and not to learn the meaning and challenge of contemporary history is to repeat the sin of the first man. (It is not an original sin, it is a common sin.)

The Bible, in having established the reality of genuine history, stressed again and again the necessity of ongoing faithfulness to the Covenant of the past. History is devoid of genuineness when acts take place in complete detachment from the commitment to the past. *Carpe diem,* the enjoyment of the present in complete isolation is defiant of history.

Genuine history occurs when the events of the present disclose the meaning of the past and offer an anticipation of the promise of the future.

History is encounter of the eternal and temporal. Just as

[1] See Abraham J. Heschel, *The Prophets* (New York: Harper & Row, 1962).

129

the Word is a veil for revelation and sign for prayer, so history may form a vessel for God's action in the world and provides the material out of which man's doing in time is fashioned.

Only rarely does the present shed light on the meaning of this encounter. But what was valid in the past concerns us at all times, and what is hidden from sight close at hand can at times be discerned from a distance.

The Spirit of God speaks intermittently through the events of history, and our life is a continual wrestling with the Spirit. Whenever our historical memory becomes dim, the forsaken Spirit shakes us, and we know once more that we are servants by the grace of God.

Our honor is given to us as pledge for fidelity to Israel. Human guilt and divine grace determine our existence. Through individuals, the people shares in guilt, and through the people individuals share in grace.

The Jewish question is a question addressed to us by God. Our existence is the history of a responsibility, and the prehistory of an answer.

The present is reunion with the past. But the future will be reunion with what is yet to be disclosed.

130

HISTORY IS NOT CONSUMED

The presence of God in history is never conceived to mean His penetration of history. God's will does not dominate the affairs of man. God's presence in history is sensed in the correspondence between promise and the events in the relation to God's promise that testify to His presence. Sacred history is the collecting of the threads of His promise.

Genuine history goes on even though it may not always be manifest or strike forth in spectacular events. The relationship of the Jewish people to the land of Israel is itself living history. Just as ardent love between human beings can be real and powerful even though they don't dwell together on one spot in space, the love of the Jewish people for the land is an ongoing, powerful being together even when living at a distance, a real link, a being at home spiritually, an embrace that never tires, a hope that never ceases.

131

Moses, tending the flock of his father-in-law, Jethro, drove the flock into the wilderness, and came to Horeb. An angel appeared to him in a blazing fire out of a bush. He gazed, and there was a bush all aflame, yet the bush was not consumed. Moses said: "I must turn aside to look at this marvelous sight; why is the bush not consumed?" (Exodus 3:1–3.)

What is the relevance of Moses' vision? Buddha under the bo-tree awoke to the realization of the impermanence of the phenomenal world. Moses at the burning bush saw a permanence that defies destruction.

The amazement of Moses: the bush was burning, yet the bush was not consumed. We too, walking in the wilderness, arrive at times at the mountain of God and see the whole world—a burning bush, aflame with hatred, envy, and murder—yet the world is not consumed.

History is like a burning bush. Though each instant must vanish to open the way to the next one, history itself is not consumed.

History is the realm of divine meaning. But where shall meaning be found in history? Hopes are wrecked, faith is mocked. What must not occur, happens. Is history, then, a distortion of what God wills, misrepresenting and defying Him? Or does God's itinerary in history lead through a maze of seeming contradictions? Is His design for justice woven of more threads than man comprehends?

The anxiety afflicting the man of our age has created a

new nightmare. Is history coming to an end? Is there reason for hope?

We are God's stake in human history. We are the dawn and the dusk, the challenge and the test. Israel reborn is a renewal of the promise. It calls for a renewal of trust in the Lord of history.

History cannot come to an end as long as the promise exists. The people in whose very being the sense of history is embedded, in whose existence the promise and the hope continue to be alive, and to whose commitments the challenges are due which have put mankind on the road toward a universal order of peace under law, is now visible as a concrete political entity and a token of order to which it owes its existence.[2]

---

[2] See Carl J. Friedrich, "Israel and the End of History," *Israel: Its Role in Civilization,* edited by Moshe Davis (New York: Harper & Row, 1956), p. 106.

LIVING TOWARD REDEMPTION

What does Israel say to us? That waiting for wonder is not in vain. For two thousand years we have prayed, suffered, waited for Zion and Jerusalem. Then came moments "marvellous in our eyes" (Psalm 118:23), moments when despair seemed to go up in smoke.

The inspiration that goes out of Zion today is the repudiation of despair and the example of renewal. The dreadful experiences of the past one hundred years, far from having poisoned us with a sense of despair, have on the contrary evoked in us the vigor of hope and of resolve for renewal.

Our very existence is a repudiation of the thought that man in history "lives toward the death." Our very existence is a witness that man must live toward redemption.

The return of the Jewish people to the land of Israel is a fact that fills us with astonishment. Who would have believed it? Who would have expected it? How vain was this expectation considered by people throughout the centuries.

The road to the establishment of the state led through

134

unbelievable events. To be sure, many Jews had to make choices and radical decisions in order to be involved in the process of upbuilding. And yet the numerous events in that process seemed to point to an intimation that history is not always made by man alone.To dwell in the land is to sense that the idols of cynicism are tottering.

Life in Israel is insight into the meaning of history. Here causation is no explanation. What we obtain is only an intimation, suggestive but not definitive. It is certainly a great occasion to live such an intimation, and meaning emerges only out of the union of living and intimation. To those who are addressed by the memory of history, the uniqueness of a moment may be the beginning of the refutation of absurdity. Despair is not man's last word. Hiddenness is not God's last act.

135

MOUNT SINAI AND MOUNT MORIAH

What brought the State of Israel into being? A stream of dreaming, the sacred river flowing in the Jewish souls of all ages. No heresy could stem it, no apostasy could defile it. The State of Israel having been born out of our soul is itself a state of our soul, a reality within us.

Judaism is not simply an amalgam of national concepts, moral and ritual laws, subjective emotions. Jewish existence is an engagement to what is greater than ourselves. It is sustained by numinous powers; it is carried on the wings of a hidden Presence in history. That Presence, often passive and suppressed, breaks forth in rare moments.

There has been a mysterious power in Jewish history which again and again came to crush occasional indifference to Zion and Jerusalem. Whenever we tend to be forgetful, history sends us a reminder.

And yet, it is so much more than a state of the soul; it is a carrying out of a divine imperative. God has led us through hell and said: Return ye to the Holy Land, children of men. So we followed His lead, and behold, "the Lord went before them in a pillar of cloud by day, to guide them along the way, and in a pillar of fire by night, to give them light" (Exodus, 13.21).

It is dangerous to regard political affairs as religious events; yet since the time of Abraham we were taught that political affairs are to be understood within the orbit of God's concern. We must not expect the history of politics to read like a history of theology. Instances of God's care in history come about in seeming disarray, in scattered fashion —we must seek to comprehend the unity of the seemingly disconnected chords.

To the eyes of the heart, it is clear that returning to the land is an event in accord with the hidden Presence in Jewish history. It is a verification of a biblical promise. It has saved so many lives, it has called forth so much dedication and sacrifice, it has revived hope. Returning to the land is an event in which the past endures, in which the future is foreshadowed.

His thoughts are not our thoughts, His ways are not our ways. But this is not always the case. At times the human and the divine meet or coincide.

Exceedingly intricate are His ways. Any attempt to formulate a theory, to stamp a dogma, to define God's itinerary through history, would be a shallowness, fraught with pretension. In the realm of theology, shallowness is treason.

137

To our conscience Israel reborn is holy. This is why in the inner chambers of our anguished souls the State of Israel is holy.

Why was Mount Moriah chosen to be the site on which to build the Temple and the Holy of Holies rather than Mount Sinai on which the Ten Commandments were given? The answer offered is that Mount Moriah was the site where Abraham sacrificed his beloved son and the sanctity of sacrifice transcends the sanctity of the Commandments.

Infinitely greater than the sacrifice of Isaac was the martyrdom of Auschwitz, Bergen-Belsen, Dachau, Treblinka, and others. The State of Israel was built on that martyrdom; its people are, to use a phrase of the prophet Zechariah (3:2), "a brand plucked from the fire."

The rescue of a people from physical oppression and even destruction from the corroding influence of assimilation . . . the reclamation of the land from the aridity and barrenness to which most of its soil had been condemned by the spoliation and neglect of man and nature, is an act of sanctification.

138

THE ALLEGORIZATION OF THE BIBLE

While it is proper and even necessary to seek to derive by a variety of interpretive methods new meaning from ancient sources, it is a fact that the attempt of traditional Christian theology to reduce concrete narratives, hopes, expectations connected with a living people and a geographic land, to paradigms of Church dogma has had detrimental results for Christian theology.

The radical use of the method of allegorization of the Hebrew Bible, the tendency to spiritualize the meaning of its works and to minimize its plain historical sense has made many Christians incapable of understanding or empathy for what the Holy Land means to the Jewish people and to the authors of the Hebrew Bible, or for what the people Israel means in the flesh, not just as a symbol or as a construct of theological speculation. Even many Christian theologians who are no longer committed to the method of allegorization react in a way as if the concrete people Israel,

139

the city of Jerusalem, the hope of the restoration of Zion, were illusory entities.

"The allegorical method essentially means the interpretation of a text in terms of something else, irrespective of what that something else is."[3] Its use in biblical exegesis which goes back to Philo has often been accompanied by the assumption that we must distinguish in Scripture a body and a soul, a literal sense and a spiritual sense. The literal sense is depreciated, the spiritual sense exalted.

The allegorical method developed by Philo has its echoes in the Epistle to the Hebrews. By the middle of the second century, allegory, though not generally used by the New Testament writers, finds acceptance in the Church, for example, in the Epistle of Barnabas, and in Justin Martyr.

Allegoric interpretation is based on the supposition that Scripture intended to express some other meaning than what is literally said. Extreme allegorization, or the exclusive nonliteral method of interpreting Scriptures, particularly when adopting neo-Platonic methods of thinking, tends to contrast the real which is heavenly and eternal with the apparent which is earthly and temporary. By such a method biblical history and laws were construed as being, in reality, mere intimations of the mysteries of faith. Over and above that, it was maintained that in the Bible the

---

[3] H. A. Wolfson, "Philo," *The Philosophy of the Church Fathers* (Cambridge: Harvard University Press, 1956), Vol. I, pp. 1, 3–4.

spirit is concealed in the letter, that the immediate and apparent meaning of the Bible is but a shadow of the mystery, the "shadow" tending to obscure the mystery. Since the Hebrew Bible was but a foreshadowing, and the New Testament a reality, it was possible to allegorize the Hebrew Bible while taking the words of the New Testament literally. While Philo used the method of allegorizing to derive from the Hebrew Bible timeless truths of philosophy, the New Testament writers sought to demonstrate that the events of the present are fulfillments of predictions contained therein. Subsequently, Christian typological exegesis saw the events of the Hebrew Bible as the prefiguration of the events in the New Testament. It saw in the facts of the Hebrew Bible something in preparation, something sketching itself out, of which the writers themselves were not aware because it lay quite beyond their purview.

"The proper motive was the firm belief that the Old Testament was a church document. For the church, the allegorical method was its primary means of making the Old Testament a church document."[4] The allegorization of the Bible became the recognized method of dealing with the Hebrew Scriptures within the Church. This method enabled the exegetes to find intimations of the life of Jesus

[4] B. Ramm, *Protestant Biblical Interpretation* (Boston: W. A. Wilde, 1956), p. 29.

neai!y everywhere. The two goats which are brought into the Sanctuary on the Day of Atonement typified the two advents of Jesus. Jacob served Laban for sheep, so Jesus became a servant so that he might purchase his flock. Moses holding up his hands during the battle with Amalek is a type of Jesus on the cross.[5]

There was also a tradition of more sober exegesis cultivated by Theodore in the Antiochene School. Epiphanius mentioned that "Scripture does not need allegory; it is as it is. What it needs is contemplation and sensitive discernment."[6]

Luther insisted that the Word of God is imparted through Scripture and that Scripture is above the Church. Yet what he meant by the Word was not the Bible itself but the divine offering itself to man. "Take Christ out of the Scripture and what else will you find in them? Understanding the Bible means finding Christ in it."[7]

It was modern critical scholarship that paved the way for the understanding of the literal and historical dimensions of the Bible that we now consider indispensable for theological understanding.

Few men today could accept the view that the mind of man created the universe as it created the principles of

[5] See *Dialogue with Trypho,* 54:1.
[6] E. C. Blackman, *Biblical Interpretation: The Old Difficulties and the New Opportunity* (London: Independent Press, 1957), p. 107.
[7] Blackman, *op. cit.,* p. 125.

logic, that the universe is a form of the mind's activity deriving its being from it, authentic and authoritative only as possessed by the mind and authorized by it. It is rather difficult to comprehend how a contemporary scholar can appreciate the insight expressed in the following statement: Jesus "created the Scripture as He created the Church; both are forms of His activity, valid as they derived their being from Him, authentic and authoritative as possessed of Him and authorized by Him." It is thus mentioned that "this christocentric understanding of the Bible is the right way of approach."[8]

"When the historical sense of a passage is once abandoned, there is wanting any sound regulative principle to govern exegesis. . . . the mystical [allegorical] method of exegesis is an unscientific and arbitrary method, reduces the Bible to obscure enigmas, undermines the authority of all interpretation, and, when taken by itself, fails to meet the apologetic necessities of time."[9]

"This I consider the first principle in prophetic interpretation," writes Davidson, "to assume that the literal meaning is *his* meaning—that he is moving among realities, not symbols, among concrete things like people, not among abstractions like *our* Church, world, etc."[10] Davidson

[8] Blackman, *op. cit.*, p. 156, quoting Farrar.
[9] Kemper Fullerton, *Prophecy and Authority* (New York: Macmillan, 1919), p. 181.
[10] Ramm, *op. cit.*, p. 168, quoting Davidson, *Old Testament Prophecy.*

143

treats with a measure of scorn those interpreters who blithely make Zion or Jerusalem the Church, and the Canaanite the enemy of the Church, and the land the promises to the Church, etc., as if the prophet moved in a world of symbols and abstractions.[11]

That "Israel has a great future is clear from Scripture as a whole. There is a large unfulfilled element in the Old Testament which demands it, unless we spiritualize it away or relinquish it as Oriental hyperbole."[12]

---

[11] Ramm, *op. cit.*, pp. 234–235. Cf. "Certainly the extreme anti-literal interpretation which considers the names Zion, Jerusalem, Israel, and the like to be mere names for the Christian Church, without reference to the people of Israel, does no justice either to the spirit of the Old Testament and its principle, or to the principles on which the apostle reasons" (*ibid.*, p. 490). The essay of Neale and Littledale (*A Commentary on the Psalms*, Vol. I, Dissertation III, "On the Mystical and Literal Interpretation of Scripture," pp. 426–470) is a perfect illustration of the sort of exegesis Davidson refers to, and also constitutes a very stout defense of the traditional mystical system of interpretation. For a more recent defense of mystical interpretation see Darwell Stone, "The Mystical Interpretation of the Old Testament," *A New Commentary on Holy Scripture*, pp. 668–697.
[12] Ramm, *op. cit.*, p. 236, quoting Davidson, ch. XXIV, "The Restoration of the Jews."

BODY AND SPIRIT

Religious existence is not limited to prayer, dogma, and observance of rituals. Hewing stones, paving roads, planting gardens, building homes, can also be carried out as prayers in the form of deeds. Seeking to conquer helplessness and infirmity, to overcome despair and despondency, are acts that forge reminders that there are deeds in which God is at home in the world.

In Judaism there is no absolute bifurcation of the secular and the religious, of the concrete and the spiritual, of the common and the marvelous. The spiritual is not the antithesis of the material. Both aspects are interrelated. We must seek to endow the material with the radiance of the spirit, to sanctify the common, to sense the marvelous in everydayness.

It was well within the spirit of classical Jewish thinking that the following statement was coined: "Body and soul are like friends and lovers to each other."[13]

13 *Midrash Ha-neelam, Zohar,* Vol. I, 134b.

145

Before God sanctified time, He created things of space. What is the meaning of living in the world of space? To master things of space in order to sanctify moments of time. Even before He blessed the Seventh Day and made it holy, God blessed man and said, "Be fertile and increase, fill the earth and master it and rule the fish of the sea, the birds of the sky, and all the living things that creep on earth" (Genesis 1:27).

Just as we are told, "Remember the Sabbath day to keep it holy," we are commanded, "Six days you shall labor" (Exodus 20:8–9). The upbuilding of the land of Israel was inspired by a new awareness of the sanctity of physical labor.

The dichotomy of spirit and letter is alien to Jewish tradition. What man does in his concrete, physical existence is directly relevant to the divine. Man is body and soul and his goal is so to live that both "his heart and his flesh should sing to the living God" (Psalm 84:3). While the soul without the body is a ghost, the body without the soul is a corpse.

The Hebrew Bible is not a book about heaven—it is a book about the earth. The Hebrew word *erets,* meaning earth, land, occurs at least five times as often in the Bible as the word *shamayim,* meaning heaven.

We will never be able to sense the meaning of heaven unless our lives on earth include the cultivation of a foretaste of heaven on earth. This may also explain why the

146

promise of the land is a central motif in biblical history. God has not given the land away—He remains the Lord and ultimate owner: "For Mine is the land" (Leviticus 25:23). Living in the Holy Land is itself a witness to the almost forgotten truth that God is the Lord and owner of all lands.

We must cultivate the earth as well as reflect on heaven. The Hebrew Bible is a book dealing with all of man, and redemption involves spiritual purification as well as moral integrity and political security.

Harmony of heaven and earth rather than their perennial tension is the hope. Everything certifies to the sublime, the unapparent working jointly with the apparent. Security, justice and renewal on earth are prerequisites to such merging. According to Rabbi Yochanan of the third century, who lived in Palestine: "The Holy One Blessed Be He said: I will not enter heavenly Jerusalem until I can enter earthly Jerusalem" (Ta'anit 5a).

The destiny of heavenly Jerusalem depends upon the destiny of Jerusalem on earth.

The agony of our people particularly in this century was dreadfully concrete and redemption of our people and all peoples, we believe, must also be concrete. It is not enough to be concerned for the life to come. Our immediate concern must be with justice and compassion in life here and now, with human dignity, welfare, and security.

IMMEDIACY OF MEANING

In contradistinction to Neo-Platonic thinking, which contrasted the real that is heavenly and eternal with the apparent that is earthly and temporary, Judaism insisted upon the deeper unity of both. Thus, the content of the Bible, its history and laws, were never dissolved in allegory nor reduced to mere shadows of heavenly ideas. Primacy is given to the immediate meaning of the words, while at the same time acknowledging the intimation of deeper meaning. Jerusalem, for example, is not only a reflection, not only an intimation and a witness to Him who transcends heaven and earth—Jerusalem and her concrete being, Jerusalem and the life of those who live in her, are the immediate spiritual challenge.

Jewish tradition, while searching for deeper meanings, insisted upon the primacy of the historic and immediate meaning of the Word. It rejected the kind of allegorization that deprives the Bible of its independent inherent life. With very few exceptions, the words of the Bible must be

148

taken in their explicit sense. "Throughout the Torah no verse loses its ordinary, plain meaning."[14]

To the biblical man, concrete reality, the world of sense perception, actual human conduct, is the immediate religious challenge. To Jewish tradition the words of the Bible are relevant, both objectively and symbolically, both historically and spiritually. Judaism involves a relationship to the immediate meaning of the words, not only a relationship to the ideas symbolized by the words. We must distinguish between symbolism as a form of religious thinking and religion as a form of symbolic thinking. The first is valid, the second is deceptive. The Bible is not only a symbol. It is above all a reality.[15]

Indeed, the books of the Bible deal not only with moral and spiritual issues. They also describe the land and its boundaries, districts and cities; they recount its history from the days of Joshua to the return from Babylon in the time of Ezra and Nehemiah. It is from the books of the Bible that historians and archaeologists derive their fundamental knowledge.

[14] Shabbath 63a; Yebamoth 11b. "A verse is not to be diverted from its obvious and generally recognized meaning except when its obvious intention is to be taken figuratively." (Saadia Gaon, *Book of Beliefs and Opinions* [New Haven: Yale University Press, 1948]. Translated by Samuel Rosenblatt, VII: 4, p. 272, fn.)
[15] See Abraham J. Heschel, *Man's Quest for God: Studies in Prayer and Symbolism* (New York: Charles Scribner's Sons, 1954), pp. 115 ff.

5

Jews,
Christians,
Arabs

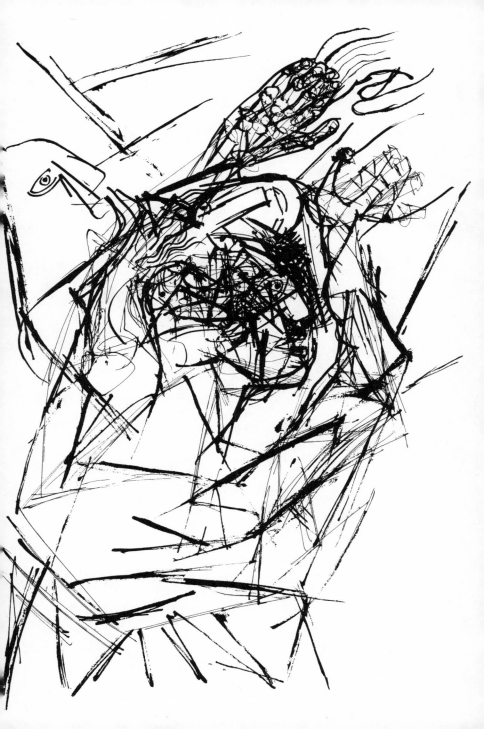

TWO LEVELS OF REDEMPTION

Jewish thinking was essentially shaped by two different perspectives each of which suggested a different way and approach to reality. One perspective may be called rational, historical, realistic, stressing the concreteness of things, human values, natural order. The other perspective, which may be called prophetic or apocalyptic, looks at the world from the point of heaven—its concern is with supernatural events, the miraculous, the indescribable, and the paradoxical.

Basic issues were conceived and defined in accordance with the perspective. The problem of Messianic redemption was equally understood from two different perspectives.

155

From the first perspective the Messianic redemption was essentially political redemption—the abolition of foreign rule and persecution and the return of the people to the land. According to the prophetic perspective, Messianic redemption was expected to be a radical transformation of the world, of the nature of man and beast, the underlying assumption being that history, human nature, all of nature, have gone astray, and the only cure is radical change in the cause of things. The other more realistic conception does not share that assumption and is thus interpreting Messianic redemption as political renewal.

The prophets predicted that in the days of the Messiah eternal peace would be established, even beasts of prey would cease to cause injury. The world would be restored to a state of innocence, there would be neither guilt nor merit.

The wolf shall dwell with the lamb,
and the leopard shall lie down with the kid,
and the calf and the lion and the fatling together,
and a little child shall lead them.
The cow and the bear shall feed;
their young shall lie down together;
and the lion shall eat straw like the ox.
The sucking child shall play over the hole of the asp,
and the weaned child shall put his hand on the
adder's den.

156

> *They shall not hurt or destroy*
> *in all my holy mountain;*
> *for the earth shall be full of knowledge of the Lord*
> *as the waters cover the sea.*

Isaiah 11:6–9

Throughout the ages the expectation prevailed that the days of the Messiah would inaugurate a new order of things, while there were individual voices who seemed to have insisted upon the words of Ecclesiastes: "What has been is what will be, and what has been done is what will be done; and there is nothing new under the sun" (1:9).

Most Jewish sages took literally the promise of the prophets that in the days of the Messiah "Nation shall not lift up sword against nation, neither shall they learn war any more" (Isaiah 2:4; Micah 4:3). In contrast, the great scholar Samuel, teacher, physician, judge, astronomer, who lived in Babylonia (165-257) is the author of this astounding statement: "The sole difference between the present and the Messianic days is deliverance from foreign powers."

In the spirit of Samuel, Maimonides writes:

Let no one think that in the days of the Messiah any of the laws of nature will be set aside, or any innovation be introduced into creation. The world will follow its normal course. The words of Isaiah: "And the wolf shall dwell with the lamb, and the leopard shall lie down with the kid"

157

(Isaiah 11:6) are to be understood figuratively, meaning that Israel will live securely among the wicked of the heathens who are likened to wolves and leopards, as it is written: "A wolf of the deserts shall destroy them, a leopard is watching over their cities" (Jeremiah 5:6). They will all accept the true religion, and will neither plunder nor destroy, and together with Israel earn a comfortable living in a legitimate way, as it is written: "And the lion shall eat straw like the ox" (Isaiah 11:7). All similar expressions used in connection with the Messianic age are metaphorical. In the days of King Messiah the full meaning of those metaphors and their allusions will become clear to all.[1]

There are two views concerning the coming of the Messianic era. The one view maintains that the redemption of Israel and the Messiah will appear suddenly from heaven, and that amid miracles and wonders he will gather the Israelites of the Diaspora to their ancient inheritance. According to the other view the beginning of the redemption will take place in a natural way by the desire of the Jews to settle in Palestine and the willingness of the nations to help them in their work.

Redemption, scholars insisted, was not to be conceived of solely as an act that will come about all at once and without preparation. It is an ongoing, continuous process in which

[1] *The Code of Maimonides, Book Fourteen, The Book of Judges.* Treatise five, Chapter XII (Yale Judaica Series, New Haven, 1949), p. 240.

all have a role to play, either retarding or enhancing the process. Not only is redemption a necessity for man, man is a necessity to redemption. His actions are vital and affect the course of that process. Man holds the key that can unlock the chains fettering the redeemer.

A central concern in Jewish thinking is to overcome the tendency to see the world in one dimension, from one perspective, to reduce history exclusively to God's actions or to man's action, either to grace or to man's initiative. The marvelous and the mundane, the sacred and the secular, are not mutually exclusive, nor are the natural and the supernatural, the temporal and the eternal, kept apart. The heart of the relationship of God and man is reciprocity, interdependence. The task is to humanize the sacred and to sanctify the secular.

In the face of apocalyptic overstatements of the supernatural aspect of Messianic expectation, it was necessary for Judaism to find a voice in Samuel of the third century and in Maimonides of the twelfth century to stress the natural, moral, and political aspect of what is meant by the Messianic age.

The two views of Messianism complement each other, manifesting the inherent polarity of Judaism and, indeed, of human existence.

The spiritual without the political is blind, the political without the spiritual is deaf. The attainment of the first is an epilogue, the attainment of the second is a prologue.

159

The task is not to abandon the natural order of creation but to purify it; to humanize the sacred, to sanctify the secular.[2]

The hope is for universal redemption, for ontological transformation. Yet it seems that fulfillment will come about by degrees.

Judaism insists upon the single deed as the instrument in dealing with evil. At the end of days, evil will be conquered by the One; in historic times evils must be conquered one by one.

"The inner history of Israel is a history of waiting for God, of waiting for His arrival. Just as Israel is certain of the reality of the Promised Land, so she is certain of the coming of 'the promised day.' She lives by a promise of 'the day of the Lord,' a day of judgment followed by redemption, when evil will be consumed and an age of glory will ensue.

"The climax of our hopes is the establishment of the kingship of God, and a passion for its realization must permeate all our thoughts. For the ultimate concern of the Jew is not personal salvation but universal redemption. Redemption is not an event that will take place all at once at 'the end of days' but a process that goes on all the time. Man's

[2] The dialectics that dominates the history of rabbinic thinking throughout the ages is the subject of my work *Theology of Ancient Judaism* (in Hebrew), published by Soncino Press (London and New York), Vol. I, 1962; Vol. II, 1965; Vol. III, in preparation.

good deeds are single acts in the long drama of redemption, and every deed counts. One must live as if the redemption of all men depended upon the devotion of one's own life. Thus life, every life, we regard as an immense opportunity to enhance the good that God has placed in His creation. And the vision of a world free of hatred and war, of world filled with understanding for God as the ocean is filled with water, the certainty of ultimate redemption, must continue to inspire our thought and action."[3]

THE CHRISTIAN APPROACH

There is little doubt that the establishment of the State of Israel came as a shock, even a scandal, to some Christians. They held that in punishment for the crucifixion of Christ the Jews would not return to their ancient homeland unless

[3] Abraham J. Heschel, *The Insecurity of Freedom* (New York: Farrar, Straus & Giroux, 1966), p. 146.

161

they came to believe in him. There was the cry of the crowd before Pilate's palace: "His blood be on us and on our children" (Matthew 27:25); there were other biblical texts—all seemed to tell of lasting exile. Thus, the present restoration, partial though it was, seemed a contradiction of the inspired word.

Examples of the belief that Scripture demanded the barring of the Jews from the Holy Land are not lacking in recent times, nor have they been confined to the market place. When in 1869 the Spanish Cortes (the legislature) debated freedom of worship, Professor Emilio Castelar took up the cause of the Jews. He was answered by Vicente de Manterola, a deputy, who advised the Jews not to rebuild the Temple in Jerusalem, not to reorganize as a people under a scepter, a flag, or a president, for the moment they succeeded, "the Catholic Church will have been slain, because the word of God will have been slain." Francisco Mateo Gago went further. In an open letter he insisted that the Jews "walk the earth" because they carry a curse; that till the last judgment they will be without a country of their own, without a fixed abode, without prince, without sacrifice. This seemed to him the clear teaching of the prophet Hosea (see 3:4).

However, there is nothing in the words of Jesus "to lead us to believe that He envisioned a physical desolation that would endure to the end of days. . . . A study of the patristic and scriptural sources makes us conclude that the

162

belief the Jews could never regain their lost nationhood did not have its origin in Scripture or in a dogmatic patristic tradition. Rather it is based on the writings of several of the Fathers of the later fourth century—principally Chrysostom—who, unduly influenced by the dramatic failure of Julian the Apostate to reconstruct the Temple, interpreted certain texts of the Old and New Testaments in the light of this event and read into them temporal specifications which an exacting exegesis cannot discover or support. Hence, the existence of a Jewish state, be it the state of Israel or another, does not contradict sacred Scripture."[4]

There is, moreover, a passage in the New Testament that seems to reflect the belief of the early Christian community in the restoration of the kingdom to the Jewish people. According to the Book of Acts, the disciples to whom Jesus presented himself alive after his passion, asked him: "Lord, is it at this time that thou restorest the kingdom to Israel?" And he said to them: "No one can know times and seasons which the Father fixed by His own authority" (Acts 1:6–7).

What is the meaning of this question and this answer? It was a time when Jerusalem was taken away from the Jewish people, the holy Temple destroyed, Jews sold into slavery. Pagan Rome ruled in the Holy Land.

[4] Edward H. Flannery, "Theological Aspects of the State of Israel," *The Bridge*, Vol. III, pp. 304, 312 ff.

But there was a hope, a hope of deliverance from the pagans, there was the promise offered by the prophets, of returning Jerusalem to the kingdom of Israel. It was the most urgent question. So when they saw Jesus for the first time in these extraordinary circumstances, it is understandable that this was the first question they asked, their supreme concern: "Is it at this time that thou restorest the kingdom?" In other words, they asked the question about the restoration.

Jesus' answer was that the times of the fulfillment of the divine promise were matters which lay within the Father's sole authority. So, earlier, he had assured them that he himself did not know the day or hour of his parousia. "But of that day or the hour [of the parousia] no one knows, not even the angels in heaven, nor the Son, but only the Father" (Mark 13:32). A similar awareness is common in Rabbinic literature. "Nobody knows when the house of David will be restored." According to Rabbi Shimeon the Lakish (*ca.* 250), "I have revealed it to my heart, but not to the angels." Jesus' answer is as characteristic of the Rabbinic mind of the age as the question.

However, this passage is generally interpreted in a different way. Reflecting a dichotomy in early Christian thinking, the position of the Galilean disciples was different from that of the Hellenistic Christians. The original hope of the disciples was that the kingdom was at hand in the apocalyptic sense, but the Hellenistic Christians, who

164

in the end conquered the empire, preached the Gospel as having present importance for each individual apart from the eschatological kingdom. True to the tendency of disregarding any secular or political relevance to the early Christian message, the question contained in this message was criticized rather than appreciated.

Thus Augustine explains the meaning of the question to be that Jesus after the resurrection was visible only to his followers, and they asked whether he would now make himself seen to everyone.[5] Calvin maintains that "there are as many errors in this question as words."[6] According to

[5] F. J. Foakes Jackson and Kirsopp Lake (eds.), *The Beginnings of Christianity* (London: Macmillan), Part I, *The Acts of the Apostles,* Vol. IV (1933), p. 8.

[6] He points out that Apostles were gathered together when this question was posed, "to show us that it was not raised through the foolishness of one or two but through the concern of all. Yet their blindness is remarkable, that when they had been so fully and carefully instructed over a period of three years, they betrayed no less ignorance than if they had never heard a word. There are as many errors in this question as words. They ask Him concerning the Kingdom; but they dream of an earthly kingdom, dependent upon wealth, luxury, outward peace and blessings of this nature. And while they assign the present as the time for restoring this Kingdom, they desire to enjoy the triumph before fighting the battle. Before setting hands to the work for which they are ordained they desire their wages; they also are mistaken in this, that they confine to Israel after the flesh the Kingdom of Christ which is to be extended to the farthest parts of the world. The whole question is at fault in this, that they desire to know things which are not right for them to know. No doubt they were well aware of what the prophets had said about the restoration of the kingdom of David, for they had often heard Christ speaking of this, and it was a common saying that in the depths of the captivity of the people every man's spirit was re-

modern commentators, the question reflects the spiritual ignorance and hardness of heart of the disciples,[7] "the darkened utterance of carnal and uninspired minds,"[8] and the answer of Jesus as a rebuke.[9]

However, the simple meaning of the entire passage has a perfect *Sitz im Leben,* and both question and answer must be understood in the spirit of their times. The Apostles were Jews and evidently shared the hope of their people of seeing the kingdom of God realized in the restoration of Israel's national independence. So now, hearing their Master speak of the new age, they asked if this was to be the occasion for restoring the kingdom to Israel. We can scarcely fail to realize or to understand the naturalness of

---

vived by the hope of the Kingdom to come. They hoped that this restoration would take place at the coming of the Messiah, and so the apostles, when they saw Christ raised from the dead, at once turned their thoughts to this. But in so doing they betrayed what poor progress they had made under so good a Master. Therefore Christ in His short reply briefly reprimands their errors one by one, as I shall presently indicate. To 'restore' in this passage means to set up again that which was broken down and disfigured by many ruins. For out of the dry stock of Jesse should spring a branch, and the tabernacle of David which was miserably laid waste should rise again." (*Calvin's Commentaries, The Acts of the Apostles,* [Edinburgh, 1965], p. 29.)

[7] "The hardness of the disciples' hearts is apparent here as in Mark's Gospel; they awaited a material kingdom, for the Spirit was not yet poured out on them to give them a more enlightened conception of it." (C. S. C. Williams, *A Commentary on the Acts of the Apostles* [London, 1964], p. 56.)

[8] G. T. Stokes, *The Acts of the Apostles* (New York, 1903), p. 29.

[9] R. B. Rackham, *The Acts of the Apostles* (London, 1901), p. 7; A. W. F. Blunt, *The Acts of the Apostles* (Oxford, 1922), p. 132.

their question. The expectation was burned into their very being by the tyranny of the Roman rule. The answer confirms the expectation that the kingdom will be restored to Israel—an expectation expressed again and again in ancient Jewish liturgy. The point in history at which that restoration will take place remains the secret of the Father.[10]

It is very likely that following Daniel and Esdras, calculations were made to predict the time of the coming of the restoration. However, most rabbis disapproved computations that dealt with the "time, two times, and half a time" of Daniel 7:25. Jesus' answer is not a rebuke of the Apostles' hope; it is, rather, a discouragement of Messianic calculations (see Luke 17:20–21).

Jesus' expectation that Jerusalem will be restored to Israel is implied in his prediction that "Jerusalem will be trodden down by the Gentiles, until the times of the Gentiles are fulfilled" (Luke 21:24). This saying announces not only the destruction of Jerusalem, but the end of Israel as a political entity as well. The Gentiles are, commentators agree, the Romans, whose armies set fire to the Temple and laid Jerusalem in ruins under Titus in A.D. 70, and who humbled her again when Hadrian, about the year 135, sought to turn her into a pagan city in the Greek style.

Some commentators, indeed, see in these words a prediction of "the re-establishment of Jerusalem as a capital of the Jewish nation."

[10] F. F. Bruce, *Commentary on the Book of the Acts* (Grand Rapids, 1954), p. 38.

167

ISLAM AND THE LAND OF ISRAEL

The biblical insistence that God granted the land of Canaan to the children of Israel is repeated in the Koran, the holy book of Islam. "We settled the Children of Israel in a beautiful dwelling-place, and provided for them sustenance of the best" (Sura X, 93). "We made a people considered weak (and of no account) inheritors of lands in both East and West—lands whereon we sent down Our blessings. The fair promise of thy Lord was fulfilled for the Children of Israel, because they had patience and constancy." (VII, 137).

In the Koran, Sura V, 4:22–23, the only passage in which the Holy Land is mentioned, we read the words of the Lord spoken to Moses and to the Jewish people, descendants of Isaac:

> *Remember Moses said*
> *To his people: "O my People!*
> *Call in remembrance the favour*
> *Of God unto you, when He*

168

Produced prophets among you,
Made you kings, and gave
You what He had not given
To any other among the peoples."

"O my people! enter
The holy land which
God hath assigned unto you,
And turn not back
Ignominiously, for then
Will ye be overthrown,
To your own ruin."

In the famous commentary (1856 edition) by Al-Za-makshari (1074–1144), we read the following interpretation:

THE HOLY LAND—Some say it is the mountain and its surroundings, and some say it is Syria. Others say it is Palestine and Damascus and a part of Urvum. Some say that God presented to Abraham this land as an inheritance for his children when he went up to the mountain and said to him: Look around as far as your gaze can reach (every place reached by your eyes will be theirs). The Holy Temple was the dwelling place of the prophets and the residence of the believers.
GOD HAS ASSIGNED IT UNTO YOU—The Lord has promised (or sworn) it to you and written in the Tablets that it is yours. Do not turn your back to it. *Turn*

169

not back—do not run away out of fear of the giants who live there.

A similar note is found in the commentary of Baidawi (thirteenth century).[11]

Down to the end of the nineteenth century, many Moslem rulers, Arab and Turk, acknowledged the special right of the Jews to enter and settle the land, in contrast to Christians, who could for the most part only visit as pilgrims.

In a book published in 1864, the Italian scholar Ermette Pierotti, who spent many years in Jerusalem, was author of a number of works on the area, and served as chief architect to the Ottoman governor, the Pasha of Jerusalem, wrote:

We all know, and the Arabs also are aware, that God said to Abraham: Unto thy seed I will give this land, and repeated the promise several times to him and to Isaac and to Jacob. So fully do the Mohammedans believe this.

Now, on 8 July 1861, the day on which the news of the death of Abdul Megid and the accession of Abdul-Azis arrived in Jerusalem, the Jews waited with all formalities on the Governor, Surraya Pasha, and requested him to restore to them the keys of Jerusalem according to a right on the death of one sultan and the accession of another. At the same time, they brought forward such proofs of the justice

[11] I owe the references to these commentaries to Professor M. Zucker.

170

of their demand that the Pasha did not refuse it but referred to his ordinary council consisting of the Mufti, or chief officer of religion, the Cadi, or chief judge, and other persons of distinction natives of the country. Their decision was in favour of the Israelites, the whole Council being aware that they were the ancient owners of the country. The ceremony was accordingly performed in the following manner. Saïd Pasha, the general of the forces, accompanied by officers of his staff and some members of the Council, and followed by a crowd of sightseers, went to the Jewish quarter where he was met by a deputation of that nation and conducted to the house of the Chief Rabbi who received the Pasha at the door and there was publicly presented with the keys.[12]

That the return of the Jews to Palestine would prove a blessing, not only to themselves but also to their Arab neighbors, was envisaged by the Emir Feisal, who was a great leader of the Arab peoples at the Peace Conference following World War I. On March 3, 1919, he wrote:

We Arabs . . . look with the deepest sympathy on the Zionist movement. Our deputation here in Paris is fully acquainted with the proposals submitted yesterday by the Zionist Organization to the Peace Conference, and we regard them as moderate and proper. We will do our best, insofar as we are concerned, to help them through. We will

[12] Ermette Pierotti, *Customs and Traditions of Palestine* (Cambridge, 1864), pp. 75 ff.

171

wish the Jews a most hearty welcome home. . . . I look forward, and my people with me look forward, to a future in which we will help you and you will help us, so that the countries in which we are mutually interested may once again take their places in the community of civilized peoples of the world.

During the Turkish era of domination of Palestine (1517–1917), many Turkish sultans looked with favor on the establishment of a large Jewish community in Palestine. In 1561, as mentioned above, Don Joseph Nasi, Duke of Naxos, a refugee from the Portuguese inquisition who had risen to high rank at the Turkish Court, obtained permission from the Sultan to rebuild the ruined city of Tiberias and to establish in it and in its rural surroundings a new Jewish settlement. The grant, issued in the name of the aged Suleiman, is said to have been countersigned by his son, Selim, the heir apparent, and by the latter's first-born and successor, Murad, as a token that it was to be valid for all time. The area in question was apparently to be set aside for Jews who were ultimately to predominate in it. It was understood that the little plot of land on the shores of Lake Tiberias was to be not merely a city of refuge but the kernel of a Jewish state, dependent of course, on the great Turkish empire.

Don Joseph sent proclamations to all parts of the Diaspora calling upon Jews to emigrate to Palestine and become

172

farmers and artisans in the new community. Owing to revolts which broke out at the time in the Lebanon and in northern Palestine, the enterprise failed to make progress, but its vestiges are still to be found in some ancient villages of Galilee.

ARABS AND ISRAEL

The Lord of history has always placed us in predicaments, and this seems to be part of our destiny, never to relax in complacency, but to face difficult tasks, to live by the challenge.

In this world there is no gem which is not in need of refinement, no wheat without chaff, no vineyard without weeds, no roses without thorns. Light and shadow are mingled. There is need of refining, rethinking.

The joy and exaltation that come from Israel reborn are mixed with pain and chagrin over the suffering and bitterness that are found in the Middle East today.

The return of the Jewish people to the land of Israel, which was first welcomed by Arabs living in the land, has, under the influence of reckless leaders, become a bone of bitter contention. At the beginning, many Arabs correctly realized that in the millions of square miles in the Middle East there was ample room for Jewish and Arab nationalism to grow in harmony in the process of achieving self-determination. The clash which subsequently occurred was due to the extremist character of Arab nationalism, a condition that continues to exist.

The thing that separates us from the Arabs is the claim of two per cent of the area of the Middle East, while the values and interests that unite us comprise 90 per cent of our personal and social being. As a result, efforts to bring about a reconciliation between Jews and Arabs, to bring about good will and readiness to cooperate by asking Arab consent to a bi-national state in Palestine, have found no response on the part of the Arab leaders. On the contrary, Jewish settlements were menaced with terror. And the intransigence of Arab leaders did not abate. The Grand Mufti of Jerusalem, Haj Mohammed Amin el-Husseini, as chairman of the Arab Supreme Council organized the Palestine disturbances in 1936 and 1937. During World War II he participated in Rashid Ali's pro-Axis coup in Iraq before going to Europe where he assisted Hitler and was largely responsible for the liquidation of the Jews in the Moslem areas of Bosnia.

174

Husseini's anti-Jewish activities date from 1920. Encouraged by British policies in Palestine, which had the effect of fostering friction and antagonism between Jews and Arabs, he launched an attack by Arab nationalists against the Jews of the Old City of Jerusalem. This was the first clash of this kind between Jews and Arabs, who had lived together peacefully in Jerusalem for hundreds of years.

The Jews in the Old City defended themselves. The British authorities, practicing a policy of "balance," punished and put under arrest both the rioters and the defenders. Soon afterward, amnesty was granted to both sides and the instigator of the riots, Haj Amin el-Husseini, upon being released from prison, was appointed by the British high commissioner to the post of Mufti of Palestine and head of the Islamic Council.

This prompted the Mufti to renew the riots the following spring (1921). A gang of Arabs started out from the Hassan Beck Mosque in Jaffa to attack the nearby Jewish homes in the area between Jaffa and the new Jewish town of Tel Aviv. Jewish defenders went forth to meet the attackers and an exchange of fire followed which threatened to develop into a full-fledged war between Jews and Arabs. It took the courage of one person to stop the riots and call an end to the disturbances, which were not renewed until eight years later, in 1929.

This man was neither a soldier nor a politician. He was a

man of the cloth, a scholar and a spiritual leader—Rabbi
Ben Zion Uziel. At that time, he was the rabbi of the small
community of Sephardic Jews in Tel Aviv. (Many years
later, he was to be elected to the post of Sephardic Chief
Rabbi of Palestine.) He himself was born in the Old City of
Jerusalem and his family had lived there for many generations. When the shooting started, Rabbi Uziel donned his
rabbinic robes and turban and went out to the battlefield.
Passing by the Jewish positions, he asked the defenders to
hold their fire for a while. Alone, he then proceeded toward
the Arabs and called out to them to halt their fire. The
sheik in command of the Arabs instructed his people to lay
down their arms for a brief respite at the request of the
Jewish Hacham. Rabbi Uziel, standing alone in the "no-
man's land" between the two fighting camps, then addressed himself thus to the Arab rioters:

"It is indeed no mere accident that this country, more
than any other country in the world, has changed hands so
many times. It has now been taken by the Allied Powers
who have agreed to make it possible for the Jews to rebuild
their ancient homeland. After they were forced to leave
this land, they have waited for hundreds of years for it to
be restored to them, accepting no other homeland.

"It is also no accident that this land of ours, which has
plagued its inhabitants with malaria, blindness, famine,
and locusts, has ever since the renewal of Jewish settlement
on it seen areas of awful desert turn into flourishing Eden.

176

New fountains of water were discovered and new vistas of abundance and prosperity were opened up for all the inhabitants of the land. These new beginnings brought about through great labor and supreme sacrifices point to the providential design to restore the children of Israel to their land. Abundant natural resources are hidden in the land. They have only begun to come to the fore, but many more will be revealed in the near future and will yield happiness and prosperity, a pleasant life and tranquility to this unique land upon which the Lord's eye stays from the beginning of the year until the end. We candidly stretch out our hand to you with true peace in our hearts and say: We have the entire land in front of us, let us work shoulder to shoulder to cultivate her, uncover her treasures, and live together in brotherhood. Know you and trust that God's word will surely be fulfilled. Make your peace with us and we shall make peace with you and together we shall enjoy God's blessings on this holy land."

Here the Rabbi paused and moved closer to the Arabs who had come out of the places of ambush and were listening attentively to his words. He now called out to them with greater enthusiasm:

"Our dear cousins! Our common father, Abraham, the father of Isaac and of Ishmael, when he saw that his nephew Lot was causing him trouble claiming there was not enough room for both his flocks and Abraham's flocks to live together, said to him: 'Let there be no quarrel between me and you, and between your shepherds and my shepherds, for we are people like brothers.' We also say to you, this land can sustain all of us and provide for us in plenty. Let us then, stop fighting each other, for we too, are people like brothers."

The Arabs who had listened to his words in silence dispersed quietly.

Throughout the ages, we have witnessed tension, conflicts, wars. In the midst of such events, the opinion prevails that the interests of the respected parties are forever irreconcilable, that Roman Catholics and Protestants, French and Germans, can never coexist in peace. Such a view was maintained in Europe after World War II about communism and the West. Yet today each camp has had to learn to live with the other as a fact of life. The Arabs will have to learn this fact of life, as the Israelis already have. The Middle East cannot remain permanently an armed jungle, with unnamed terrors lurking on each side. Men of good will never cease to pray that the logic of peace may prevail over the epidemics of suspicion.

Arab leaders claim that the State of Israel is responsible for the Arab refugee problem. However, according to indisputable and abundant evidence, the refugee traffic was largely stimulated and encouraged by Arab leadership itself.

The exodus from Israel, begun when fighting broke out

after the passing of the United Nations Resolution of November 29, 1947, was hastened and enlarged by the invasion. Villagers and townsfolk were exhorted by their leaders to withdraw "temporarily" to neighboring territories and clear the way for the advancing columns.

Anxious as they were for an orderly and peaceful transition to statehood, the Jewish authorities did what they could to arrest the exodus. Israel's Proclamation of Independence called upon "the sons of the Arab people dwelling in Israel to keep the peace and to play their part in building the State, on the basis of full and equal citizenship and due representation in all its institutions, provisional and permanent." Appeals in similar phrasing were circulated by every available means—radio, handbills, soundtrucks.

In Haifa, from which the first large-scale flight took place, the British Police reported to Jerusalem Headquarters on April 26, 1948: "Every effort is being made by the Jews to persuade the Arab population to stay and carry on with their normal lives, to get their shops and businesses open and to be assured that their lives and interests will be safe."

Thrice in two decades, Arab armies have made war against the State of Israel, only to be repulsed. In each instance their declared aim has been the destruction of the Jewish state—an aim consistently reasserted and three times actually attempted.

The Arab refugee was born out of this design. He is the

179

victim of a barren policy conceived by his own leaders. Had there been no wars against Israel—in 1948, in 1956, and again in 1967—there would not be a single Arab refugee today. Once brought into being, however, the Arab governments have, for twenty years, used the Arab refugee as a prime political weapon in their campaign against Israel. Every proposal for his absorption and rehabilitation—and there have been many—has been killed so as to guarantee that the refugee problem should live on, endlessly, as a tool of propaganda and hatred. That many thousands of the refugees have, nevertheless, succeeded in breaking out of the sterile existence to which they have been condemned remains a source of official Arab displeasure.

In its first nineteen years, Israel has given sanctuary and home to a million and a quarter Jewish refugees. Almost half that figure come from Arab League countries. The Jewish refugees who came to Israel from the Middle East and North Africa left, for the most part, under the direct impact of official threats and persecution. This was not a new phenomenon. Throughout the 1930's and 1940's, a steady stream of Jewish refugees came to mandated Palestine from Iraq and Yemen as a result of the disabilities and, at times, persecution to which they were subjected. Their number was joined by Jews from Egypt and Syria, who saw no future for their children in the climate of growing extremism.

In 1947, the Arab leaders stepped up their threats

180

against their local Jewish communities. During the debates in the United Nations General Assembly in 1947, preceding the UN Resolution on the establishment of a Jewish state, the head of the Egyptian delegation did not hesitate to warn that international body that "the lives of a million Jews in Moslem countries will be jeopardized by the establishment of the Jewish State." Jamal al-Husseini, Chairman of the Palestine Arab Higher Executive, spoke in a similar vein. "If a Jewish State were established in Palestine," he said, "the position of the Jews in the Arab countries would become very precarious," adding the ominous warning that "Governments have always been unable to prevent mob excitement and violence."

The number of the Jewish refugees is, thus, of roughly the same order of magnitude as the number of the Arabs whom the League's invasion of Israel in 1948 induced to depart. Seen in its total effect, this constitutes a legitimate population exchange. The major difference—and a very material one—is that in the case of the Jews who came to Israel they were totally and constructively absorbed into the country, the financial burden being borne mainly by the State of Israel and the Jewish people. In the case of the Arab refugees, however, a strict policy designed to keep them uprooted has been pursued, with the inevitable result that they have remained an object of international charity, the burden of support falling upon the United Nations and the international relief agencies. The plight of these refugees has been turned by Arab propaganda into a great international issue, while the outside world has hardly become aware of the mass exodus of the Jews from the Arab countries.

The fact that the ultimate guilt for the Arab refugees lies with their leaders does not absolve us of the responsibility for their plight. It is clear that the Jewish people in Israel as well as the Jews everywhere are most eager to contribute generously toward a just and charitable solution to this human tragedy. It is also clear that the rulers of the neighboring states have seen in the continuation of the refugee problem a weapon to be used against the State of Israel.

On June 29, 1967, the government of Israel issued a statement on the Arab refugee question in these terms: "With the creation of the new conditions in the region, there now exists a situation permitting a general and immediate solution to the refugee problem, with regional and international cooperation."

It is, of course, obvious that the extent of Israel's success in launching this program will depend, ultimately, upon the degree of regional and international cooperation forthcoming.

Arab and Jew are more than neighbors. They share the fact of kinship.

Israel reborn is bound to be a blessing to the Arab world,

182

to play a major role in their renaissance. The Arabs and the Israelis must be brought into mutual dependence by the supply of each other's wants. There is no other way of counteracting the antagonism.

The Jews of Israel are not an outpost of any foreign domination. Their ambition is to integrate themselves into the modern structure of reviving Asia. At the same time, they are anxious to make their contribution to the great work of bridge-building between modern Asia and the rest of the world. They claim what is the natural right of any people on the face of the earth—that as many of them as possible should live together in their own country, freely develop their civilization, make their contribution to the common stock of humanity, and be self-governing and independent.

There is no greater fallacy than to regard Israel as a "colonial" phenomenon. No state in the world expresses the concept of nationhood more intensely than Israel. It is the only state which bears the same name, speaks the same tongue, upholds the same faith, inhabits the same land as it did 3,000 years ago. Recently a group of young Israelis near the Dead Sea came across some parchment scrolls written 1900 years ago. They are entirely intelligible to a young citizen of Israel today. Israel is not alien to the Middle East, but an organic part of its texture and memory. The long separation has had less effect on the region's history than the original birth and the modern renewal.

183

Take Israel and all that has emanated from Israel out of Middle Eastern history—and you evacuate that history of its central experiences. Arab political and intellectual leaders have never made a serious effort to understand, even in reluctant mood, the tenacity, depth and authenticity of Israel as a national reality with deep roots in the Middle East.[13]

In peaceful conditions we could imagine communications running from Haifa to Beirut and Damascus in the North; to Amman and beyond in the East; and to Cairo in the South. The opening of these blocked arteries would stimulate the life, thought and commerce of the region beyond any level otherwise conceivable. Across the Southern Negev communication between the Nile Valley and the Fertile Crescent could be resumed without any change in political jurisdiction. What is now often described as a wedge between Arab lands would become a bridge. The Kingdom of Jordan, now cut off from its natural maritime outlet, could freely import and export its goods on the Israeli coast. On the Red Sea, cooperative action could expedite the port developments at Elath and Aqaba which give Israel and Jordan their contact with a resurgent East Africa and a developing Asia.

The Middle East, lying athwart three continents, could become a busy center of air communications, which are now impeded by boycotts and the necessity to take circuitous routes. Radio, telephone and postal communications which now end abruptly in mid-air would unite a divided

[13] Abba Eban, "Reality and Vision in the Middle East," *Foreign Affairs* (July, 1965), p. 633.

184

region. The Middle East with its historic monuments and scenic beauty could attract a vast movement of travellers and pilgrims if existing impediments were removed. Resources which lie across national frontiers—the minerals of the Dead Sea and the phosphates of the Negev and the Aqaba—could be developed in mutual interchange of technical knowledge.

Economic cooperation in agricultural and industrial development could lead to supranational arrangements like those which mark the European Community. The United Nations could establish an Economic Commission for the Middle East, similar to the Commissions now at work in Europe, Latin America and the Far East. The specialized agencies could intensify their support of health and educational development with greater efficiency if a regional harmony were attained. The development of arid zones, the desalination of water and the conquest of tropical disease are common interests of the entire region, congenial to a sharing of knowledge and experience.

In the institutions of scientific research and higher education on both sides of the frontiers, young Israelis and Arabs could join in a mutual discourse of learning. The old prejudices could be replaced by a new comprehension and respect, born of a reciprocal dialogue in the intellectual domain. In such a Middle East, military budgets would spontaneously find a less exacting point of equilibrium. Excessive sums devoted to security could be diverted to development projects.

Thus, in full respect of the region's diversity, an entirely new story, never known or told before, would unfold across the Eastern Mediterranean. For the first time in history, no

185

Mediterranean nation is in subjection. All are endowed with sovereign freedom. The challenge now is to use this freedom for creative growth.[14]

The purpose of politics is to serve the ordered progress of society along the lines of greatest usefulness and convenience to itself. The present situation in the Middle East represents a supreme example of political perversion.

We all must ask the nations of the Middle East: Drop your antagonisms and your antipathies, your hatred and your fears, and seek to think in terms of one family. The alternative to peace is disaster. The choice is to love together or to perish together. Let the love of life have the final word.

The fatal disease that is infecting many minds today is politics as an isolated, autonomous science following its own rules, unhampered by moral consideration or respect for truth. Politics should be part of an all-embracing effort to preserve, to enhance, to ennoble the most sacred thing on earth—human life. Politics bears upon eternal relationships. It is doomed unless carried out within a confrontation with the moral question. It deals with human beings, not with beasts; with people, not with computers. The pestilence of our day is the dehumanization of politics.

Power is not its own end. It turns demonic when de-

[14] From an address by Abba Eban in the General Assembly of the United Nations on June 19, 1967.

tached from moral meaning, from moral commitment. Politics, the use of power, turns self-destructive when defying truth. The intemperate pragmatism that prevails in the approach to the state and its values tends to obscure its real meaning. Many Arabs are prisoners of a blind hatred, and hatred is self-defeating. It is the true enemy of the Arabs. Years of fighting, years of terror have caused dreadful harm, perverted political and social thinking.

The State of Israel is a necessity of history. All it asks of the Arabs is acknowledgment of its right to exist. Arab intransigence is responsible for the continuation of suffering and terror.

We have a right to demand, "Love thy neighbor as thyself." We have no right to demand, "Love thy neighbor and kill thyself." No moral teacher has ever asserted, "If one stands with a knife threatening to kill you, bare your heart for him to murder you." There is no moral justification for self-destruction.

The Middle East has excellent prospects for an intellectual revival, comparable to the time when the famous seats of learning, Alexandria, Beirut and Antioch, flourished beside the Jewish academies of Palestine, or when, six hundred years later Jewish, Christian and Moslem scholars could engage in Baghdad in free dialogue and discussion of problems of philosophy and theology. The tradition of Jewish-Arab cooperation is ancient and rich. The Holy Book of Islam, the Koran, contains a huge mass of material which

187

can be traced to Jewish (as well as Christian) sources, not only of biblical and apocryphal literature but also elements from Jewish liturgy and later law. Adolf von Harnack characterized Islam "as recast of the Jewish religion on Arab soil."[15]

Scholars speak of a great Jewish-Arab symbiosis manifested in the influence of Judaism in the creation of Mohammed and on the subsequent development of Islam as well as in the diverse ways in which Arab Moslem civilization affected Judaism and even Hebrew literature. Greek science and Greek methods of thinking made their entrance into Jewish life mainly through the gate of Arab Moslem literature.

The most perfect expression of Arab-Jewish symbiosis is found in the Hebrew poetry in Moslem countries, particularly in Spain. Religious poetry had been a very important branch of Hebrew literature before Islam, yet it was due to the influence of Arabic that the secular Hebrew poetry came into being, was cherished and preserved. "Thus, it was the influence of Arabic on Hebrew which made the rise of medieval Hebrew poetry possible."[16]

The Arabs and the Jews in addition to having a common background and history, early contacts and a prolonged and fertile symbiosis during the Middle Ages, have also another

[15] Quoted in S. D. Goitein, *Jews and Arabs* (New York: Schocken Books, 1964), pp. 46 f.
[16] Goitein, *op. cit.*, p. 156.

affinity in common: a heritage of suffering and humiliation.

Many factors have contributed to the cultural and economic stagnation of the Middle East.

The revival of Israel and the resurgence of the Arabs, which came about in the twentieth century, face numerous problems. Cooperation of both nations is a vital necessity for both and will undoubtedly prove a blessing for both.

189

6
A rendezvous
with history

I will restore
people Israel,
rebuild the
and inhabit them
vineyards and they
wine, and they
gardens and
I will plant
their land,

the fortunes of my
and they shall
ruined cities
they shall plant
and drink their
shall makes
eat their fruit.
them upon
and they
shall
never
again

be
plucked
up out
of the
land,

which
I
have given
them,"

says the
Lord your
God."
(AMOS 9:14-15)

A RENDEZVOUS WITH HISTORY

Between the middle of May and the middle of June, 1967, the Jewish people had "a rendezvous with history." We have lived through days of anguish and through days of wonder. Many of us discovered the inner face of our being. It is important to recall the moments of anguish before probing the meaning of the moments of wonder.

The Syrians and Egyptians, Jordanians, Iraqis, Algerians and Saudi Arabians, with their intense hatred, combined for a war of extermination. A Psalm of Asaph was on our lips, a psalm that read as if it were written in May, 1967.

195

O God, do not keep silence;
do not hold thy peace or be still, O God!
For lo, thy enemies are in tumult;
those who hate thee have raised their heads.
They lay crafty plans against thy people;
they consult together against thy protected ones.
They say, "Come, let us wipe them out as a nation;
let the name of Israel be remembered no more!"
Yea, they conspire with one accord;
against thee they make a covenant—
the tents of Edom and the Ishmaelites,
Moab and the Hagrites,
Gebal and Ammon and Amalek,
Philistia with the inhabitants of Tyre;
Assyria has also joined them;
They are the strong arm of the children of Lot. . . .
Let them know that thou alone,
whose name is the Lord,
art the Most High over all the earth.

Psalm 83:2–9, 19, rsv, 83:1–8, 18

This psalm was our continuous prayer for weeks, while
we were witnessing how the Arab rulers were forging a
ring of vast armies, tanks, and planes around Israel, an-
nouncing the blockade of the Gulf of Aqaba, proclaiming a
"holy war" of extermination.

Terror and *dread* fell upon Jews everywhere. *Will God*

196

permit our people to perish? Will there be another Auschwitz, another Dachau, another Treblinka?

The people in the land of our fathers are "the remnant
of Israel and the survivors of the house of Jacob" (Isaiah
10:20), "a brand plucked from the fire" (Zechariah 3:2),
survivors of Nazi extermination camps. Will God permit
"Israel, his first-born son" (Exodus 4:22) to be destroyed?

The darkness of Auschwitz is still upon us, its memory is
a torment forever. In the midst of that thick darkness there
is one gleam of light: the return of our people to Zion. Will
He permit this gleam to be smothered?

The spirit of those days was like the spirit of the Days of
Awe in the life of Jewish piety, like the moment when the
Day of Atonement is about to arrive, when in fear and
trembling one knows that his soul is on trial and one's life
is as naught, unless one repents and is reprieved by forgive-
ness and pardon. In those days many of us felt that our own
lives were in the balance of life and death and not only the
security of those who dwelt in the land; that indeed all of
the Bible, all of Jewish history was at stake, the vision of
redemption, the drama that began with Abraham.

Some of us felt that those were days of judgment for the
Holy One of Israel. Will He desert us? Will He hide His
face again? Some people maintained that should Israel
suffer a defeat, they would commit suicide . . . .

This intense distress which affected one's total being, the
roots of the self, was more than sympathy. It was the real-

197

ization that the soil in which the very meaning of our existence is rooted may be taken away from us that rocked us to the depths. I felt that my soul and history were one.

To those in affliction the Shekinah says: "When he calls me, I will answer him; I will be with him in trouble . . ." (Psalm 91:15), and Jews in the world said to the people of Israel: Our own life is bound up with yours.

But the world stood still. The world that was silent while six million died, was silent again, save for individual friends. The anxiety was grueling, the isolation was dreadful. "A nation that dwells alone" (Numbers 23:9).

It was more than a state of emotion. It was a time of hearing a demand. Our ears, which have heard again and again the prayer on the Sabbath, "Take pity on Zion, for it is the House of our Life," perceived the demand. Even those of rugged insensibility felt called upon to respond. Every one of us heard the voice: "Where art Thou?" and every one answered: "Here I am." Insights that persuasion could not instill were suddenly driven home by awesome moments.

Many speculations, discussions, books, and essays have dealt with the question of why it is significant to be a Jew. What speculation did not accomplish, history brought about. We felt all of Jewish history present in a moment.

It was an awesome time, the collapse of all complacency. All cynicism came to an end. Flippancy ceased, indifference stopped. The days stood still, ages resurrected, converging. All exiles trembling within me, Abraham insisting, Rachel pleading.

As an individual I discovered that I am a wave in the mysterious movement of Jewish history. Israel is the premise, I am the conclusion. Without the premise, I am a fallacy. I had not known how deeply Jewish I was. The Bible, we discovered, lives within us, reverberates in our anxiety. Our involvement with the prayers and the loyalties of all ages became powerfully apparent. The Bible, we discovered, is not a book that is sealed and completed; the Bible lives, always being written, continuously proclaimed (see above, "The Bible Is Our Destiny"). In those days of distress a Christian friend asked me, "Why are you so dreadfully upset, so dreadfully desperate?" I answered, "Imagine that in the entire world there remains one copy of the Bible and suddenly I see a brutal hand seize this copy, the only one in the world, and prepare to cast it into the flames . . . ."

The dreadful anxiety passed, the *memory* of that dreadful anxiety will never pass. It will not be easily erased from our conscience. It was a moment of purification and spiritual self-identification. The walls fell, the walls that separated the diverse parts of our people. The love of Israel swept us all with no distinction between near and far, believer and nonbeliever. Suffering can be ennobling—if it is remembered. The commandment of faith in the Torah is *Remember*: "that you may remember the day of your departure from the land of Egypt as long as you live" (Deuteronomy 16:3).

"Take utmost care and watch yourselves scrupulously, so that you may not forget the things that you saw with your own eyes and so that they do not fade from your mind as long as you live, and make them known to your children and to your children's children: the day you stood before the Lord your God at Horeb. . . ." (Deuteronomy 4:9–10).

200

Remember . . . remember. My people, do not forget: the days of distress and the days of wonder, the abyss of distress and the treasures of wonder.

A great moment is like a miracle, and we are taught that it is wrong to rely on miracles. Nor is it proper to depend on good intentions. Even those sages who maintain that good deeds do not require good intentions, and are precious in themselves, would certainly concede that good intentions require good deeds. "The road to hell is paved with good intentions." The great moment, the good intention, is like a flash. Important and vital as such a moment is, it is equally necessary to perpetuate that flash and live by a steady shining of the spirit. How to perpetuate the flash? How shall a degree of that enthusiasm continue? How to direct the memory of the deep anxiety of those days into an ongoing response to the challenge of the land of Israel, and to personal effort and involvement in the building of the land?

The anguish of those awesome days and the amazement of the events that followed demand of us a review of our attitudes and the re-examination of our views. After the days of exultation come the days of relaxation. It is beyond the power of man to live in continuous tension. Peace has not arrived, difficult hours are ahead of us.

201

A RE-EXAMINATION

What part did the State of Israel play in the day-to-day life of the Jews outside the land until the recent events? It was a footnote to one's existence enjoyed as a fringe benefit, a nice addendum, a side dish, a source of self-congratulation and pride. Israel was a place to visit, a place of pleasure and tourism, not a challenge, not a voice demanding meditation, not an urging for spiritual renewal, for moral re-examination. We have been occupied with many vitally important issues. We disregarded the challenge of Israel. We have failed to clarify its meaning, its value to our existence. We have failed to convey its significance to our Christian friends.

The major weakness was to take the State of Israel for granted, to cease to wonder at the marvel of its sheer being. Even the extraordinary tends to be forgotten. Familiarity destroys the sense of surprise. We have been beset by a case of spiritual amnesia. We forgot the daring, the labor, the courage of the seers of the State of Israel, of the

202

builders and pioneers. We forgot the pain, the suffering, the hurt, the anguish, and the anxiety which preceded the rise of the state. We forgot the awful pangs of birth, the holiness of the deed, the dedication of the spirit. We saw the Hilton and forgot Tel Hai.

The land rebuilt became a matter of routine, the land as a home was taken for granted.

The younger generation seeing the state functioning normally has the impression that this has been the case all along. They have no notion of the distress and strain, of the longing and dreaming of generations. The miracle of Israel became a state like all states, with neither mystery nor sacrifice permeating it.

Habit is our downfall, a defeat of the spirit. It is habit which wrecks the soul. Living by habit is destruction of creativity. He who prays today only because he prayed yesterday—a scoundrel is superior to him, says Rabbi Mendel of Kotsk.

There is another error in understanding the situation of the State of Israel. Many people assumed the condition of the State of Israel was absolutely assured, as if the effort of building had ended, the roads cleared, the task completed. People were ready to celebrate a completion rather than realizing that the economic, political, and spiritual development is still in a stage of beginning. The achievements are impressive, but the tasks are still immense. The creation of the State of Israel was like the miracle of dividing the Red

203

Sea, and the state is still in the dry passages, in the midst of the sea. The State of Israel is a spiritual revolution, not a one-time event, but an ongoing revolution.

Not in one generation did the Yishuv (modern Jewish community of Palestine) arise, and not in one generation will the vision evolve, but at this very hour, so exalted, when Jerusalem is shedding her robes of widowhood, we must hear the voice speaking in Jerusalem from the prophet's thought.

> *Thus says the Lord:*
> *"Stand by the roads, and look,*
> *   and ask for the ancient paths,*
> *where the good way is; and walk in it,*
> *   and find rest for your souls."*
>
> Jeremiah 6:16

When Israel approached Sinai, God lifted up the mountain and held it up over their heads, saying, "Either you accept the Torah or be crushed beneath this mountain."

During the days of distress we felt as if the mountain of history was again over our heads—that either we accept our commitment to Zion or we are crushed beneath the mountain.

A supreme test in Jewish history has been imposed upon us. The eyes of all our martyrs of the past, the eyes of all Jewish generations of the future, are upon us.

We face a decisive hour in Jewish history as well as a

204

radical trial of our character and integrity as Jews. It calls
for more than generosity; it calls for wisdom and sacrifice.

A SPIRITUAL UNDERGROUND

How should one interpret the intensity of concern and
distress that overtook people who had estranged themselves
from Judaism? Why did the Arab threat of extermination
evoke such intense anguish?

Conflicts and developments taking place on many levels
impress contemporary man as involving relative justice.

> *Justice is turned back,*
>   *and righteousness stands afar off;*
> *for truth has fallen in the public squares,*
>   *and uprightness cannot enter.*
> *Truth is lacking,*
>   *and he who departs from evil*
>   *makes himself a prey.*

Isaiah 59:14–15

205

Many political issues which claim our involvement are afflicted with a degree of ambiguity. In this crisis the issue was clear and lucid: the brutal threat and the deadly danger to the existence of a people and a state. There was no shred of a doubt that the State of Israel desired peace while the Arab states proclaimed a holy war of extermination. It was justice and compassion that stirred the spirit.

However, it was not justice as an abstract principle which stirred us so deeply. Auschwitz is in our veins. It abides in the throbbing of our hearts. It burns in our imagination. It trembles in our conscience. We, the generation that witnessed the holocaust, should stand by calmly while rulers proclaim their intention to bring about a new holocaust?

A new life in Israel has bestowed a sense of joy upon Jews everywhere, by creating a society based on liberty, equality and justice, by the great moral accomplishments, by their scientific, technical and economic contributions. In the land of Israel those rescued from the holocaust of Europe and the refugees from persecution in Arab lands have found a home and are able to renew their lives.

A well which had been blocked and sealed in some deep corner of the soul was suddenly opened. What sprang forth was the realization that while we may be extending our lives in so many different directions, our secret roots are near the well, in the covenants, with the community of Israel. This is not an ideology, a matter of choice, it is an existential engagement, a matter of destiny. We may not

206

all understand the meaning of the divine but to us our relationship to the community of Israel can never be detached from our gropings for the divine.

This profound shock did not transpire in a vacuum, *ex nihilo*. It must be regarded as the outcome of the labor and influence of scholars and writers, rabbis and teachers, dedicated to the education of generations, to teaching and guiding.

Out of poverty and misery, masses of Jews came to the United States of America. There were many voices foretelling the future with self-assurance that the end was assimilation and disappearance. Voices that always negate, discourage, dishearten the old and the young. But there is always a faithful remnant eager to plant seeds and to wait.

"When they came, he looked on Eliab and thought, 'Surely the Lord's anointed is before him.' But the Lord said to Samuel, 'Do not look on his appearance or on the height of his stature, . . . for the Lord sees not as man sees; man looks on the outward appearance, but the Lord looks on the heart' " (I Samuel 16:6–7).

In those great days we discovered a spiritual underground in the hearts of the Jews of America. "Surely the Lord is in this place"; and so many of us "did not know it" (Genesis 28:16).

207

GRATITUDE

Today, we recall the promise that speaks to us from the words of the prophets: "As in the days when you came out of the land of Egypt, I will show him marvelous things" (Micah 7:15).

This is a great moment in Jewish history. With the help of God, Israel was delivered, Jerusalem is open to us. The spirit of the people of Israel is now the object of admiration, and a deepening of the sense of meaning of being a Jew has taken place in the hearts of Jews everywhere.

Who has believed what we have heard?
And to whom has the arm of the Lord been revealed?

Isaiah 53:1

The gates of the soul were opened and out of the events emerged an insight. It dawned upon many of us that biblical history is alive, that chapters of the Bible are being written.

208

> *The Lord roars from Zion,*
>   *and utters his voice from Jerusalem;* . . .
> *Surely the Lord God does nothing,*
>   *without revealing his secret*
>   *to his servants.*

Amos 1:2; 3:7

It was as if every one of us was echoing that roaring, finding within himself the mystery of being involved with the people that dwells in Zion.

The God who hides himself, went forth from His place of hiding. Must God apologize for His audacity in performing wonders in 1967?

This is the work of Providence and who is to say that there is nothing new under the sun? The heart does not grasp what the eyes perceive. We do not comprehend the surprise, we cannot fathom the mystery. We do not sanctify our lives, in accordance with God's mercy. We can only pray: "that you and your children may endure, in the land that the Lord swore to your fathers to give to them, as long as there is a heaven over the earth" (Deuteronomy 11:21). May there be heaven on earth.

Those of us who were in the land following the end of hostilities walked in amazement, in silent gratitude, overwhelmed and spellbound. In our eyes it was as if the prophets of ancient Israel had risen from their graves and walked through the streets of Jerusalem. How to welcome them? What should we say to them?

We were carried away by an awakening of the soul, overwhelmed by a vision of the profound seriousness of Jewish history. Suddenly, we sensed the link between the Jews of this generation and the people of the time of the prophets. Despite the distance of time and the difference of cultures, we are that very same living people, parts of the body of Israel of all generations.

In the days that have just passed even the unlettered among us saw that which Ezekiel could not see. Every one of us had a moment in which he said, "This is my God and I will praise him, my father's God and I will exalt Him" (Exodus 15:2).

The land of Israel is not like other lands, the people of Israel is unique. Our ideals must not become wooden, our hearts must never turn to stone. "What is in your mind shall never happen—the thought, 'Let us be like the nations, like the tribes of the countries, and worship wood and stone' " (Ezekiel 20:32).

A COMMUNITY OF CONCERN

The qualities which have been manifested in the days of crisis, qualities of care and readiness for sacrifice, are the fruit of religious discipline and the dedication in everyday life over the course of centuries. Jewish tradition, too, is the homeland.

What is the meaning of community, of fellowship among men? Community means community of concern, sharing joy as well as anxiety. At that moment of crisis it was good to witness such a community of concern among Jews, as well as among many non-Jews, for the situation of the Jews of Israel.

There is a cure of the souls in the concern on the part of the Jews everywhere for the people who live in the State of Israel. The state may be thousands of miles away, but the care we feel is intimate and strong. Such care may serve as an example to all mankind. To be concerned for the security and well-being of man everywhere is a concern that we

211

must cultivate all the time, without qualification. Wherever a man is harmed, we are all hurt.

The way that leads out of the darkness is peace between brothers, care for our fellow man. To care for our brother ardently, actively, is a way of worshiping God, a way of loving God. The clash between fathers and sons does not occupy much place in the Bible. Signs of the Oedipus complex rarely appear in the history of Israel. In the view of the Bible, the conflict which brings chaos down upon the world is hatred among brothers, fraternal hatred: the enmity between Cain and Abel, the tension between Ishmael and Isaac, between Esau and Jacob. What were the happenings which poisoned the nation and the history of Israel? The selling of Joseph by his brothers, the disputes and clashes among the tribes, the enmity and division between Judah and Israel, between Jerusalem and Samaria. It was a hatred without cause that brought about the destruction of the Second Temple. It will be love without cause that will save Israel and all mankind (Rabbi A. J. Cook).

PEACE

Bloodshed has always been an abomination to our people. For nearly two thousand years we have not lifted a sword. We have abhorred and continue to abhor violence. We have been taught by the Bible: "For not by might shall man prevail" (I Samuel 2:9).

When the leader of Nazi Germany announced his intention to exterminate our people, we did not believe it. Such evil was too staggering, inconceivable. The holocaust met us unprepared.

In May, 1967, after nineteen years of fulminating threats to exterminate the people of the State of Israel, the ruler of Egypt and his allies mobilized vast armies equipped with deadly weapons supplied by Soviet Russia. A war of extermination was about to be unleashed, the death sentence was proclaimed, what was there to be done? To disbelieve Nasser the way we disbelieved Hitler?

It was an awesome time, for me a breakthrough of realizing how deeply immersed I am in what is going on in the

213

land of Israel. Israel's very existence was in jeopardy. Threatening proclamations emanated daily from the Arab leaders.

One of the insights learned from the great crisis in May, 1967, is the deep personal involvement of every Jew in the existence of Israel. It is not a matter of philanthropy or general charity but of spiritual identification. It is such personal relationship to Israel upon which one's dignity as a Jew is articulated.

Our attitude was not sympathy or compassion.

We were ourselves in the crisis.

It would be dreadful callousness to forget that war is a nightmare, that war is hell. Whose ear can be deaf to the agony of those who were killed, maimed, injured? Whose ear can be deaf to the cries of mothers and wives whose sons and husbands will never come home? The Lord's compassion is over all that He has made (see Psalm 145:9).

We mourn the loss of lives, the devastation, the fruits of violence. We mourn the deaths of Jews, Christians, Moslems. The screams of anguish are not to be lost to our conscience.

When the Egyptians who had enslaved the children of Israel were sinking in the Red Sea, the angels were jubilant and wanted to sing a song of praise and triumph. But God, the Father of all men, said to the angels: "My creatures are drowning—and you sing!" (Megillah 10b).

The spirit that moves the people of Israel even in the

trying period of waging a war came to expression in an
address delivered by the Israeli Chief of Staff, General
Yizhak Rabin, a few days following the end of the six-day
war.

The joy of our soldiers is incomplete and their celebra-
tions are marred by sorrow and shock. There are some who
abstain from all celebration. The men in the front lines
were witness not only to the glory of victory, but the price
of victory; their comrades who fell beside them bleeding.
The terrible price which our enemies paid touched the
hearts of many of our men as well. It may be that the
Jewish people never learned and never accustomed itself to
feel the triumph of conquest and victory, and we receive it
with mixed feelings.[1]

Had God permitted Sennacherib to conquer Jerusalem
and to destroy and to disperse the people the way he dealt
with other peoples in that area, or had the Maccabees been

[1] Compare *Siach Lohamim* ("Soldiers' Talk"), a book published about
half a year after the war. It is a collection of transcripts of recorded
conversations with more than a hundred young men who fought in the
war. Many of the soldiers expressed deep concern over the moral questions, uneasiness about being a "conquering army," and found little
pleasure in their victory, just relief. One of the men said: "I believe
that one of the things characteristic of us is the sense of the tragedy of
conquerors. We are just not used to it. And it is also part of our education. . . . I am glad that I could stand on the ruins of the Egyptian
armor and that no Egyptian was seen anywhere between Beersheba
and Yeruham. But all the same, when you watch it all, it is destruction,
and it is depressing."

215

defeated, where would the world be today? There would have been no Jewish people, no Jesus, no Apostles, no Mohammed.

Sacred history has not come to an end. Many of God's blessings are still in store for all mankind. The State of Israel is a prelude, we hope, to new wonders, to new blessings.

The State of Israel from the very beginning sought peace and desired peace. During many years its voice calling for peace and cooperation was a voice calling in the wilderness. "I am for peace—but when I speak they are for war" (Psalm 120:7). Again and again was the State of Israel thrust into war against her will, in self-defense confronted with the choice to be or to cease to be. It is our ardent hope and prayer that the hour may come soon for an open dialogue between Israel and the Arabs to create reconciliation and to enter a covenant of brotherhood.The mood of this hour is gratitude. Israel continues to seek friendship and cooperation with Arab nations.

But the Arab states have consistently refused to recognize Israel's existence, have subjected it to military harassment, infiltrating the land and killing civilians. They have received arms from Soviet Russia in the amount of almost $4 billion—and the avowed purpose proclaimed by the Arab rulers was to throw the population of Israel into the sea.

Israel, we declare before all mankind, did not want a

war. The war was forced upon Israel by the Arab rulers. For Israel it was a war to thwart the design of the Arab rulers to exterminate the people of Israel, an act of self-defense.

Our aim must be to help in bringing about peace and reconciliation. Violence postpones problems, it does not solve them. We believe that by good will and full cooperation among all the nations of the Middle East, contructive solutions will be found.

How to communicate these supreme moments of amazement to all hours of our life? How to channel the experience of exaltation and gratitude into a lasting commitment to God, Torah, and Israel?

A source of deep religious insight has opened in our hearts. "The word of our God endures forever" (Isaiah 40:8). Will our sense of awe and amazement endure forever?

History is not a blind alley, we believe, and there is always a way that leads out of stupidity and sin. Over all the darkness of experience hovers the vision of a different day.

"In that day there shall be a highway from Egypt to Assyria: The Assyrian will come to Egypt, and the Egyptian into Assyria, and the Egyptians will worship with the Assyrians. In that day Israel shall be a third with Egypt and Assyria, a blessing in the midst of the earth, which the

217

Lord of hosts has blessed, saying Blessed be my people Egypt and Assyria, the work of my hands, and Israel, my inheritance" (Isaiah 19:23–25).

In the days of the prophet Isaiah, Egypt and Assyria were locked in deadly wars. Hating each other, they were both the enemies of Israel. How did Isaiah, the son of a people which cherishes the privilege of being called by the Lord "My inheritance," feel about Egypt and Assyria? The God of Israel is also the God of Syria, the God of Egypt. The enmity between the nations will turn to friendship. They will live together when they serve together. This is our hope, our prayer, our goal (see Zephaniah 3:9).

The six days of war must receive their ultimate meaning from the seventh day, which is peace and celebration.

218

MEANING

What is the meaning of the State of Israel? No single answer can exhaust its meaning. One fact is clear. In no other community do we witness such an intense, ongoing search, such an effort to understand itself in terms of a higher vision as in Israel. Mere self-preservation is regarded as an inadequate motivation.

Who can fail to sense glory in the reality of a people restored, of a people regaining its dignity, after having been defamed and marked for destruction?

In anticipation of the return to the land the psalmist sings:

When the Lord brought the exiles back to Zion
we were like those who dream.

Psalm 126:1

We have not even begun to fathom the meaning of this great event. We do not fully grasp its message for us as a community and as individuals. It has not penetrated our capacity for representing its meaning in our daily lives.

The primary religious problem in Israel is how to articulate in deeds, in living the commitment that there is an echo of God in history, trust in the prophet's word:

> *The grass withers, the flower fades;*
> *but the word of our God shall stand forever.*

Isaiah 40:8

For all who read the Hebrew Bible with biblical eyes the State of Israel is a solemn intimation of God's trace in history. It is not fulfillment of the promise, it is not the answer to all the bitter issues. Its spiritual significance, however, is radiant. Ultimately the significance of history must be understood in terms of theology.

It would be a distortion to reduce the meaning of Israel reborn to the necessity to deal with Jewish misery. It was above all the power of promise, the power of hope, that necessitated the resurrection of Israel. In a deeper sense, Israel reborn is a necessity of world history.

The wonder of the risen Israel and the gratitude to Him who has raised martyred Israel from the dead belong together. We are witnesses of the resurrection. And being a witness is a transformation.

The return to the land is a profound indication of the

possibility of redemption for all men. Stand still and behold! The unbelievable has come about.The vision was a divine promise, and the way was paved with sacrifices.

Our return to Zion is a major event within the mysterious history that began with a lonely man—Abraham— whose destiny was to be a blessing to all nations, and our irreducible commitment is to assert that promise and that destiny: to be a blessing to all nations. . . .

The central act at a Jewish wedding ceremony is the groom's saying to the bride: "Behold thou art consecrated unto me with this ring according to the Laws of Moses and of Israel." Said Rabbi Mendel of Kotsk, "If the groom says this formula but fails to say the two words 'Unto me' the whole wedding ceremony, including the meal, the music and the dancing are devoid of meaning. The essence of the entire meaning is in the words 'Unto me.' "

The return to the land: marvelous and precious as is life in freedom, its deeper meaning is in the eternal hope of the Jewish people. . . . "Unto me."

The word which Isaiah the son of Amoz saw
concerning Judah and Jerusalem.
It shall come to pass in the latter days
that the mountain of the house of the Lord
shall be established as the highest of the mountains,
and shall be raised above the hills;
and all the nations shall flow to it,
and many peoples shall come, and say:

221

> "Come, let us go up to the mountain of the Lord,
>   to the house of the God of Jacob;
> that he may teach us his ways
>   and that we may walk in his paths."
> For out of Zion shall go forth the law,
>   and the word of the Lord from Jerusalem.
> He shall judge between the nations,
>   and shall decide for many peoples;
> and they shall beat their swords into plowshares,
>   and their spears into pruning hooks;
> nation shall not lift up sword against nation,
> neither shall they learn war any more.

Isaiah 2:1–4

But that word will not go forth from Jerusalem unless all of us—Jews and non-Jews—have tasted profoundly the intensity of a waiting for the word. The burden is upon us Jews but we will not and must not do it alone. All of us must learn how to create in this dreadful emptiness of our lives, how to be illumined by a hope despite disaster and dismay.

The Bible is an unfinished drama. Our being in the land is a chapter of an encompassing, meaning-bestowing drama. It involves sharing the consciousness of the ancient biblical dwellers in the land, a sense of carrying out the biblical legacy. It is like the ladder of Jacob pointing to Jerusalem on high.

222

The State of Israel is not the fulfillment of the Messianic promise, but it makes the Messianic promise plausible. Even while our faith is fading, the power of biblical words, of biblical promise, is challenging, pursuing. Israel will abide as long as the power of the biblical word prevails.

The crisis in Judaism goes beyond the issues of creed and observance. Even if we could reach a consensus on theology and law, the question of the adequacy of present-day ethics and observance would remain. Are personal observance and traditional study, are synagogue and Hebrew schools, attuned to the earnest wrestling with the issues of massive obtuseness and the dying of the hearts? Are customs and ceremonies, are services and sermons, an adequate antidote to the massive dehumanization, to the emerging monsters of absurdity? Is Judaism as presently understood equipped to confront the challenge of the world?

Genuine history is enshrined in our rituals. Yet, ritual, loyalty, theology, remain deficient unless there is an ongoing responsiveness to the outbursts and to the demands of immediate history, of our own situations.

The integrity of our lives is determined by seeing ourselves as part of the historic context in which we live. Failure to be open to the demands of our historical situation liquidates one's own position of meaning. In order to be *responsible*, we must learn how to be *responsive*.

But many of us are like actors who recite their roles in a drama but are too deaf to hear what they say. At this

223

moment we find ourselves in a historic situation which cries for understanding as well as for participation on all levels of existence. There is no excuse for abstention or evasion.

The house is in flames and the clock ticks on.

To be is to go on, to continue, to adhere to, to carry out today what we carried out yesterday. Yet mere continuation of being leads to disintegration. Being alive means being exposed to contradictions and defiance, facing challenge and disappointment. Religion may die when its truth becomes trite—its poetry a conceit, its observance inane. Truth becomes half-truth; worship, comfort; belief, vapid.

The return to Zion is a creative challenge to stabilization, shaking up inertia, a challenge demanding new action, new thinking.

Well-adjusted people think that faith is an answer to all human problems. In truth, however, faith is a challenge to all human answers. Faith is a consuming fire, consuming all pretensions. To have faith is to be in labor.

Well-meaning people used to say that a Jewish state would be an answer to all Jewish questions. In truth, however, the State of Israel is a challenge to many of our answers. To be involved in the life of Israel is to be in labor.

What is the meaning of the State of Israel? *Its sheer being is the message.* The life in the land of Israel today is a rehearsal, a test, a challenge to all of us. Not living in the land, nonparticipation in the drama, is a source of embarrassment.

Israel is a personal challenge, a personal religious issue. It is a call to every one of us as an individual, a call which one cannot answer vicariously. It is at the same time a message of meaning, a way of dealing with the monsters of absurdity, a hope for a new appreciation of being human.

The ultimate meaning of the State of Israel must be seen in terms of the vision of the prophets: the redemption of all men. The religious duty of the Jew is to participate in the process of continuous redemption, in seeing that justice prevails over power, that awareness of God penetrates human understanding.

Jacob did not ascend the ladder but he had a vision of it. Daily a voice demands that we ascend, that we rise. Most of the time we seek the ladder and cannot find it, but there is no choice—we must cherish the vision and seek the ladder. As we have said of Israel above, its sheer being is the message. The message is a reminder of that which surpasses being. To be or not to be is not the question. We all want to be. How to be and how not to be is the essence of the question. This is the challenge we face. The Bible is the challenge and the way.

There are no easy roads, there is no simple advice. The world is dislocated, out of balance. The way of Israel is a way of rising to the peak of the mountain. At Sinai we were told, "Beware of going up the mountain and touching the border of it" (Exodus 19:12). This was interpreted by

225

Rabbi Mendel of Kotsk to mean: "Beware of going up the mountain if you have no desire ever to reach the peak." Don't play with the mountain.

The vision of reaching the peak gives meaning to our touching its border.

INDEX OF PERSONS AND PLACES

Abdul-Azis, 170
Abdul Megid, 170
Abel (biblical), 212
Abraham (biblical), 15, 31, 53, 67, 105, 128, 137, 169, 177, 199, 221
Abraham Ibn Ezra, Rabbi, 22
Abravanel, Don Isaac, 114
Abu Isa of Ispahan, 74
Abulafia of Messina, 74
Acre (Galilee), 69
Alexandria, No. Africa, 187
Al-Harizi, 120
Al-Husseini, Jamal, 181
Alroy, David, 74
Al-Zamakshari, 169
Amalek (biblical), 17, 142
Amman, Jordan, 184
Amos (prophet), 15
Amsterdam, Netherlands, 75

Antioch, Asia Minor, 187
Aqaba, Gulf of, 184, 185, 196
Ashkelon, Palestine, 69
Augustine of Hippo, 165
Auschwitz, Germany, 6, 17, 20, 111, 112, 113, 115, 138, 197, 206

Babylon, 31, 149
Baghdad, Iraq, 187
Baidawi, Abdallah ibn-Umar, 170
Bar Kochba, Simon, 59
Beilis, 106
Beirut, Lebanon, 184, 187
Benjamin of Tudela (*Itinerary of Benjamin of Tudela*), 69, 70n
Bergen-Belsen, Germany, 17, 113, 138
Blackman, E. C. (*Biblical Interpretation*), 142n

227

Blunt, A. W. F. (*The Acts of the Apostles*), 166n
Bruce, F. F. (*Commentary on the Book of Acts*), 167n

Cain (biblical), 212
Cairo, Egypt, 184
Calvin, John, 165
Castelar, Prof. Emilio, 162
Chamberlain, Joseph, 81
Chmielnicki, 94, 107
Chrysostom, John, 107, 163
Cook, Rabbi A. J., 212
Cordovero, Rabbi Moshe, 87
Cresson, Warder, 79
Cyrus the Great, 53

Dachau, Germany, 17, 113, 197
Damascus, Syria, 184
David, King, 17, 22, 28, 32, 33, 34, 52, 64–65
Davis, Moshe (*Israel: Its Role in Civilization*), 133n
Disraeli, Benjamin, 80
Dreyfus, Alfred, 106
Dumas, Alexandre (younger), 81

Eban, Abba, 186n
Elath, Israel, 184
El-Husseini Haj Mohammed Amin (Grand Mufti of Jerusalem), 174, 175
Eliot, George, 81
Epiphanius, 142
Esau (biblical), 212
Ezekiel (prophet), 15, 51, 53, 210
Ezra (biblical), 149

Feisal, Emir, 171
Flannery, Edward H. (*The Bridge*), 163n
Friedrich, Carl J. (*Israel: Its Role in Civilization*), 133n
Fullerton, Kemper (*Prophecy and Authority*), 143n

Gaon, Saadia (*Book of Beliefs and Opinions*), 149n
Gaza, 69
Gershom, Rabbi, 23
Godfrey of Bouillon, 22
Goiton, S. D. (*Jews and Arabs*), 188n
Gomorrah, Palestine, 128

Hadrian, Emperor, 167
Haifa, Israel, 69, 179, 184
Halevi, Yehudah, 61
Haman (biblical), 17
Hamburg, Germany, 75
Harnack, Adolf von, 188
Herzl, Theodor, 81
Heschel, Abraham J., 11n, 60n, 99n, 114n, 129n, 149n, 161n
Hess, Moses, 81
Hill, Marvin Sidney, 78n
Hillel, 7
Hitler, Adolf, 174, 213
Hosea (prophet), 15
Hyde, Orson, 78n

Isaac (biblical), 15, 112, 138, 177, 212
Isaiah (prophet), 15, 53, 218, 221
Ismael (biblical), 177, 212

Jackson, E. J. Foakes (*The Beginnings of Christianity*), 165n
Jacob (biblical), 15, 71, 142, 197, 212, 222, 225
Jaffa, Israel, 69, 95, 175
Jeremiah (prophet), 15
Jerusalem, Israel, 5–38 *passim*, 59, 61, 62–66, 67–68, 175, 176, 179, 212, 215, 222
Jesus of Nazareth, 141–142, 143, 162, 164, 165, 167, 216
Joseph (biblical), 212
Joseph, Duke of Naxos, 71, 172
Joshua (biblical), 67, 149
Julian the Apostate, 163

228

Jurieux, Pierre, 76
Justin Martyr, 140

Laban (biblical), 142
Lake, Kirsopp (*The Beginnings of Christianity*), 165n
Lemmlein, Asher, 74
Ligne, Prince de, 76
London, England, 75
Lot (biblical), 177
Louis XIV of France, 76
Luria, Rabbi I., 87
Luther, Martin, 142

Maccabees, 53, 215
Maimonides, Moses, 72–73, 157, 158n
Manterola, Vicente de, 162
Mateo Gago, Francisco, 162
Mendel of Kotsk, Rabbi, 203, 221, 226
Micah (prophet), 15
Mohammed, 216
Molcho, Solomon, 74
Montefiore, Sir Moses, 79
More, Sir Thomas, 81
Moriah, Mount, 138
Morse, Arthur D. (*While Six Million Died*), 108n
Moses (biblical), 11, 53, 66, 117, 132, 142, 220
Moses of Crete, 74
Murad, 172

Nahman, Rabbi, 16
Napoleon, 76
Nasi, Joseph, *see* Joseph, Duke of Naxos
Nasser, G. A., 213
Negev desert, 184, 185
Nehemiah (biblical), 53, 149
Noah, Mordecai Emanuel, 78

Oliphant, Sir Lawrence, 79

Palmerston, Lord, 79, 80
Paulli, 76
Pekiin, Galilee, 71
Philo, 140–141
Pierotti, Ermette (*Customs and Traditions of Palestine*), 170, 171n
Pinsker, Leo, 81
Poliakov, Leon (*Harvest of Hate*), 108n

Rabin, Gen. Yizhak, 215
Rachel (biblical), 199
Rackham, R. B. (*The Acts of the Apostles*), 166n
Ramlah, 69
Ramm, B. (*Protestant Biblical Interpretation*), 141n, 143n, 144n
Rashid Ali, 174
Reines, Rabbi J. J., 54n
Reubeni, David, 74, 75–76
Rifkind, Isaac (*Jewish Money in Folkways, Cultural History and Folklore*), 88n
Roosevelt, Franklin D., 108
Roth, Cecil, 71n
Rousseau, Jean Jacques, 47
Royce, Josiah (*Lectures on Modern Idealism*), 10n

Sachar, Harry, 82n
Safed, Galilee, 71, 87
Saïd, Pasha, 171
Saladin, 22
Samaria, 53, 212
Samuel (biblical), 207
Samuel (of Babylonia), 157
Schechter, S. (*Studies in Judaism*), 65n
Selim, 172
Sennacherib, 215
Serenus of Syria, 74
Shaftesbury, 7th Earl of, 79

Shimeon the Lakish, Rabbi, 164
Shulhan Arukh, 57
Sinai, Mount, 11, 45, 138, 204, 225
Sodom, Palestine, 128
Solomon, 10, 36
Stokes, G. T. (*The Acts of the Apostles*), 166n
Suleiman, 172
Surraya Pasha, 170

Tel Aviv, Israel, 175, 176
Theodore (Antiochene School), 142
Tiberias, Galilee, 71, 79, 172
Titus, Emperor, 22, 107, 167

Torquemada, Juan de, 107
Treblinka, Poland, 17, 138, 197

Uziel, Rabbi Ben Zion, 176

William III of England, 76
Williams, C. S. C. (*A Commentary on the Acts of the Apostles*), 166n
Wilson, Woodrow, 83
Wolfson, H. A., 140n

Yaari, Abraham (*Sheluhei Erets Israel*), 87n
Yochanan, Rabbi, 147

Zevi, Sabbatai, 75

230

INDEX OF PASSAGES CITED

Hebrew Bible

Genesis 1:27,	146	23:9,	198
14:18,	31	23:11,	103
18:22,	128		
22:14,	31	Deuteronomy 1:35,	103
26:3,	103	4:9–10,	200
28:16,	207	11:12,	8–9
		11:21,	209
Exodus 3:1–3,	132	16:3,	200
4:22,	197	32:43,	73
13:1,	103		
13:21,	137	I Samuel 2:9,	213
15:2,	210	16:6–7,	207
19:12,	225	26:19,	73
20:8–9,	146		
		II Samuel 12:7,	128
Leviticus 25:23,	147		
		I Kings 8:12,	10n
Numbers 14:23,	103	8:27,	10n
14:29 ff.	66		

Hebrew Bible (*cont.*)

8:41–43,	36	Hosea 2:17,	95
11:36,	12n	3:4,	162
Isaiah 2:1–4,	222	Amos 1:2,	209
2:2–4,	7, 34	3:7,	209
2:4,	157	7:17,	73
6:3,	8, 10	9:14–15,	102
8:17,	97		
10:20,	197	Micah 4:3,	157
11:6, 7,	158	7:15,	208
11:6–9,	156–157		
19:23–25,	218	Habakkuk 2:3,	97
25:6–9,	100		
25:7–8,	13	Zephaniah 3:9,	218
30:18,	97		
33:20–21,	37	Zechariah 2:10,	29
33:24,	73	3:2,	138, 197
35:1,	118	8:3,	37
35:3,	114	8:3–8,	102–103
40:1–2,	15		
40:8,	217, 220	Psalms 15,	35
43:12,	45	24:3–4,	35
52:9,	15	48:8,	12n
52:9–10,	17	83:2–9, 19,	196
53:1,	208	84:3,	107, 146
55:4,	20	87:1–7,	12
56:7,	38	90:4,	20
59:14–15,	205	91:15,	198
64:3, 4,	96	95:1,	16
65:19,	15	102:15,	15, 73
66:10,	29	118:23,	134
		120:7,	216
Jeremiah 3:17,	36, 38	126:1,	219
5:6,	158	130:1–2, 5–6	98
6:16,	204	137:1–6,	31–32
9:1,	25	137:5,	6, 15, 66–67
14:8,	95	137:6,	6
23:24,	10	145:9,	214
31:15–17,	27		
		Job 2:9,	112
Ezekiel 11:19,	98	13:15,	17, 112
13:9,	73		
20:32,	210	Lamentations 2:5,	10, 22
37:1–14,	109–110	3:10–17,	21–22

232

Hebrew Bible (*cont.*)
Ecclesiastes 1:9,   157
    3:14,   128

Daniel 7:25,   167
    12:12,   97

Nehemiah 3:34,   116
    4:2,   116

Pseudepigrapha
Baruch 4:9,   15n
II Baruch 3:1,   15n

Rabbinical Writings
Yerushalmi Berachoth 3d, 65n
Ta'anit 5a, 147
Bab. Berachoth 3b, 65n
Bab Shabbath 31a, 97
  63a, 149n
Megillah 10b, 214
Yebamoth 11b, 149n

Gen. Rabba 98, 2, 98n
Deut. Rabba 1, 12, 96n
Midrash Tehilim 22.8, 65n
Yelkut Hamakizi
  (Ps. 147:4), 15n
Zohar 1, 134b, 145n
  1, 193b, 61n

New Testament
Matthew 27:25, 162
Mark 13:32, 164
Luke 17:20–21, 167
  21:24, 167
Acts 1:6–7, 163
Hebrews 11:9, 103

Other Scriptures
Koran, Sura V, 4:22–23, 168
  Sura VIII, 137, 168
  Sura X, 93, 168